Sow the Wind

Scripture quotations in this publication are from the following versions:

KING JAMES VERSION

TLB, THE LIVING BIBLE, copyright 1971 by Tyndale House Publishers, Wheaton, Ill. Used by permission.

RSV, REVISED STANDARD VERSION OF THE BIBLE, copyrighted 1946, 1952, © 1971, 1973 Used by permission.

PHILLIPS: FOUR PROPHETS © J. B. Phillips 1963 Reprinted with permission of Macmillan Publishing Co., New York, N.Y. and Collins Publishers, London, England

Printed and bound in the United States of America.

ISBN Number 0-9603298-0-3

Sow the Wind

by VIRGINIA CORFIELD

THE PROVIDENT PRESS
Box 1112
COVINA, CALIFORNIA 91722

To the "faithful few" who prayed this book into being.

Other books by Virginia Corfield
REAP THE WHIRLWIND
THE DISCOVERY ROOM

A PROPHET-SHARING VENTURE

A while ago something happened that utterly fascinated me. At the time, I was reading the Will Durant STORY OF CIVILIZATION books each evening, and was constantly amazed to see the close parallels between the ancient world and our present day. More than once the time lines of the past blurred in my mind as I picked up a morning newspaper—only to find printed inside the same "news" I had read as history the night before. To be sure names, dates and places were changed, but little more. It was as though I were reading a reprint of the past!

This then was the beginning, *but only the beginning,* of an idea that was to capture my mind. For in addition to past and present history (as seen in secular writings), a third factor soon presented itself: THE WORD OF GOD. It just "so happened" that during the day I was also studying the Prophets of Israel: those Old Testament stalwarts who voiced in no uncertain terms God's Word relative to the day in which they lived. I was even more impressed! Here was still another period of history with the same print-out. *Only this time there was a divine editorial on what I read!*

So there I was—with bits and pieces of historical this and that, past and present, sacred and profane, sublime and ridiculous— all clamoring for mind space. *I felt as though a giant jigsaw puzzle had been overturned on me, and I was to pick up the pieces, sort them out and make sense out of them.* But where should I start? And if and when I succeeded in putting the puzzle together, what would it show me? I turned aside to see.

I started with the Word of God—cross-referencing verses, chapters, subject matter, categories. I researched the life and times of the prophets, all the while keeping an eye on contemporary historical trends. *I began to live the prophet's message!* While I was outlining the section on drought, a water **shortage hit our area; during the writing of "The Bread Line,"** inflation began to escalate. *Needless to say, I was impressed.* In the midst of "Acts of God," a major earthquake rocked Los Angeles. *I got the message!* So it went. Pieces of the puzzle were gradually falling into place, "here a little, there a little." The "Dream World" sequence brought me face to face with reality; "The Grace God" brought me face to face with God. Portions of "No Hiding Place" struck me funny; "A Song of Grief" broke my heart. *A picture was emerging.*

I was fascinated, but disturbed by what I saw. There were too many parallels for comfort, especially between the Northern Kingdom of Israel and America today. The "link ups" were inescapable. Both nations had been dearly loved of God and enjoyed great blessings. Both nations had "sown the wind" of unfaithfulness and gone out from under their God to become enamored with strange gods, strange lifestyles and strange ways. Both societies were plagued with social ills, corruption in high places, greed, violence, instability, alienation, apathy. Both lands suffered ecological woes.

At first, I was overwhelmed. The warning to America implicit in the timeless message of the prophets was only too clear. It could not be set aside. But neither could I pass by the grace of God, *for in these same messages are to be found hope and healing for our land.* America need not go the way of ancient Israel. Our history is not yet blotted and bound in a book. We can yet return to God as a nation.

But will we? I have no way of knowing. That part of the puzzle is missing. The future is still in our hands. But I do know this—a personal level, one to one, grass-roots prophet-sharing venture among the people of God; indeed, a nationwide proclaiming of the message of the prophets in the highways and byways across the land, is desperately needed. God has spoken. This is it. Our response (or reaction) to His Word will determine the way in which the puzzle is completed.

To this end, SOW THE WIND, based on the Book of Amos and REAP THE WHIRLWIND (a companion book based on the prophet Hosea), are dedicated. They are not to be read and shelved — but read and heeded. Now.

CONTENTS

BASED ON THE BOOK OF AMOS

THE VOICEPRINT OF GOD

". . . the LORD said to me, 'Go, prophesy to my people Israel'"
(Amos 7:15b, RSV).

He was a lowly man. A day laborer from an obscure village, a migrant rutted in the narrow economic pathways of the Judean wilds. In the spring of the year, he went to the plains of the Negeb to dress wild sycamore trees; piercing the low-grade fruit (to release the insect infestation) before picking it. Other seasons he herded sheep, following the flock along bleak pasture lands, shepherd's crook in hand.

Like King David, his forefather of well over two hundred years, he fought off wild beasts. Like John the Baptist, who was to follow some eight hundred years later, he lived off the barren land.

He was a true son of the wilderness—*the lay of the land was the lay of his soul.* Extremes of clear strong sunlight and dense forbidding darkness imprinted his thoughts with black and white absolutes. Lofty mountain ranges, deep-set gorges and sweeping desert wastes landscaped his heart with grandeur.

The restless interplay of burning heat with numbing cold, full-orbed sun with howling storm and stone dry wadi with torrential flood weathered his ways.

He was as rugged as the terrain, as bracing as the crisp clean air, as free of spirit as the thermal-gliding birds of passage overhead.

He was an uncommon man, this Amos. Keen of intellect, insightful, discerning of the issues of the day. Other men might be

1

deceived by the glamor of the world outside his wilderness home, *but not Amos.* Other men might be taken in by the sophistication of the hour: the golden age prosperity of the nearby Northern Kingdom of Israel, the "beautiful people" at ease on Samaria's glittering heights, the cosmopolitan shopping centers, the peaceful Middle East scene, *but not Amos.*

Others might blindly pass by the telltale cracks already visible in the integrity of the national structure: corruption in the court of King Jeroboam II, great tumults in the streets of Samaria, oppression in the market place, *but not Amos.* Others might cover their eyes with a flimsy "God will do nothing" security blanket, *but not Amos.*

With God-given vision he saw the truth about Israel: unless she returned to God, she would die.

As a patriot, Amos was troubled. But what could he do? He was not a prophet, nor the son of a prophet. He had no authority, no voice, no following (the only protest march God had called him to lead was a band of four-footed woollies). In himself, he could do nothing. So he stayed with his sheep and waited on God.

Then one day, God called Amos from the sheepcote. He called him not to do, *but to be.* Not to speak for himself, *but to be the divine voice,* God's voice of warning to the careless, sinning nation. "Go, prophesy to my people Israel."

Leaving his herds in Tekoa, Amos journeyed the dusty caravan routes to the Northern Kingdom of Israel. He went without hesitation, without question. He took one Book, one Authority, one message only. "The lion has roared; who will not fear? The Lord GOD has spoken; who can but prophesy?"

The divine thrust unerringly guided him to the ornate pagan temple at Bethel, the cathedral city of the apostate land. Up before the idolatrous high priest of the golden calves he strode. Undaunted and unbowed. Unawed by the assembled leaders of the land. *Had he not come at God's command?*

Was he not God's man at Bethel?

There he stood, a lone dissenter. A David before Goliath; a rough-hewn rustic in an ecclesiastical wilderness.

As a mightly lion in the forest roars his territorial rights, so he thundered the outraged holiness of a sovereign God. As a skilled laborer dresses the fruit of the sycamore, so he ripped open the low-grade men of Israel—piercing their pride, tearing the scales from their eyes, seeking their release from the infestation of evil.

As though rounding up strays, he sought to bring God's wayward flock to repentance while there was yet time.

THE VOICEPRINT OF GOD

"Seek the LORD and live . . ."

He was the voiceprint of God. Nothing more, nothing less. A verbal handwriting on the wall. A faithful reproduction of the whole counsel of God. A visual graph-like image, a spectograph of the very words of God to a backsliding nation.

The words that he spoke were faithful and true to the divine essence. With bold strokes they charted the very thought patterns of the God with whom Israel had to do. Line upon line, precept upon precept; with black and white clarity they delineated her true condition, with straight-ahead camera-shot candor they focused her need.

Amos added no inflection of his own, left no impression not of God. The image he gave was clear and unblurred. Usable in every detail. Emphasis, accent, pitch, frequency, intensity—all duplicated the original print transcribed in the written Word of God.

His was an authentic voice. If Israel had chosen to continue as a "nation under God," she would have matched his print and made a positive identification. She would have returned to the LORD her God and lived.

But as it was . . .

SAMARIA THE BEAUTIFUL

". . . Samaria. so famous and popular among the people of Israel" (Amos 6:1b, TLB).

THE LOUNGE SET
IVORY PALACES
THE FOREMOST NATION
NUMBER ONE
THE LIBERATED COWS

THE LOUNGE SET

"Woe to those lounging in luxury at Jerusalem and Samaria, so famous and popular among the people of Israel " (Amos 6:1, TLB).

Even today the "good life" beckons . . .

Life was sweet in Israel. Honey dripped from beehived rocks. Terraced hillside vineyards flowed vintage wines. Well-laden olive trees ran rivers of oil. The sun shone, the rains came and the earth yielded a ground swell of rich crops and abundant harvests. Granaries overflowed, the economy flourished and prosperity spread over the land like a green bay tree.

But that was not all. Life was sweet, and the living was easy. Not since King Solomon's heyday had the Israel scene boasted such rich overlays of opulence and wealth. Throughout the length and breadth of Palestine, all a man might ever wish for was his for the taking.

The "good life" had come.

In the Southern Kingdom of Israel, Jerusalem was the place to be. Jerusalem, the royal home of the kings of Judah, the throbbing center of court intrigue, the "famous and popular" darling of the beautiful people of the day. Everybody of importance in the Southern Kingdom could be found in Jerusalem at the height of the social season: seeing and being seen at lavish parties, indulging expensive tastes for the finer things in life, reveling in sunny days and balmy evenings, luxuriously at ease.

Yet for all this, Jerusalem was not the only place to be. For even as Judah lounged on Mount Zion, sunning herself like a stretched-out lizard on the warm limestone rocks, Ephraim (her sister nation to the north) lounged on the cool Samaria hills—curled up in the lap of luxury like a sleek fat cat, well-fed and well-heeled, smug and self-satisfied.

And well might Ephraim purr with self-satisfaction, and even a sense of superiority over her sibling rival. For anything Judah had, Ephraim had more in abundance; anything Judah could do, Ephraim could do better. Whatever sophistication, whatever degree of elegance, whatever culture found in the Southern Country; the Northern, with its proximity to the international trade routes far exceeded.

To be sure, Jerusalem might be the City of God, but all roads led to Samaria, the city-capital of Ephraim.

And why not? Was she not "Samaria the Beautiful"? The pride and joy of the kings of Northern Israel?

Was she not the "Great Crown Jewel" of the Middle East? The fabulous ivory inlay on the Fertile Crescent green belt?

She was all that, and much more. Poised and secure atop a proud hill, and situated not too far from the Great Trunk Road that linked Egypt with Mesopotamia, she played a glamorous role in the passing scene of her day. For Samaria was every inch a star. Gay, witty, charming. Utterly enchanting. A fascinating companion; a much sought-after cosmopolite. A gracious hostess-city.

In adoration the ancient world beat a path to her door. Well-worn caravan trails from exotic climes humbly interchanged at her feet. Traveling luminaries from throughout the fabled East lodged overnight within her fortress walls. Suitor nations vied for her favors. Foreign affairs brought tribute to her throne.

Even fashion bowed before the dictates of her taste. In a *haute couture* world, where multiple changes of apparel doubled as status symbols, the stylish women of Samaria reigned supreme. Whatever milady's whim—whether a deceptively simple daytime frock, a resort wear casual, a new silhouette . . . perhaps a modified tent, a caftan float, or a softly shirred bit of feminine fluff (complimented by delicately woven sandals adorned with narrowed straps and tinkling ankle bells); whether king's ransom finery, avant-garde elegance, or a head-held-high attempt to update last year's wardrobe; whatever, wherever, however—the latest, the finest, the most daring innovations fresh from the designer's sketch pad belonged to the sensuous lovelies of Samaria.

Let the Jerusalem-based prophet Isaiah decry the haughty "daughters of Zion" with their stretched forth necks and mincing steps. They were but provincial schoolgirls beside the daughters of Jezebel!

Without a doubt, Samaria was where the action was. She was a city constantly in motion; a pleasure dome revolving around its structured social set. From dawn till dusk there was always something to keep heads whirling—always something new under the sun.

For those able to rise to the occasion, the early morning hours offered an ancient-world bouquet of environmental delights: lilies of the field arrayed in sun-splashed glory, picture-postcard views of distant green-ridged heights, glimpses of Mediterranean blue beyond Mount Carmel's wooded shoulder—clear skies, brilliant light, sparkling transparent air, the lilting rise of crested larks to greet the sun, the swift power dive of sharp-eyed eagles, the mournful voice of sleepy turtledoves.

Not to be outdone by nature, the beautiful people began their social rounds with a garland of festive morning affairs. As the warm-up sounds of a new day were heard in the land, they enjoyed *al fresco* dining in the courtyard, garden parties set amid ornamental shrubs and potted palms, even royal receptions staged on the palace pleasure grounds—all gatherings being graced with attendants outnumbering the celebrity-studded guest lists, and a full measure of strolling musicians, groaning banquet tables and well-stocked bars.

Obviously, the early bird may have had his worm, but the high-living Israelites had everthing else!

But this was only the beginning . . .

As the sun rose higher, the day's pace quickened. There was always some "fun" thing, some "in" thing for the lounge set to do. Then there were endless "must" things, as well.

For the ladies, there were fittings to be squeezed in, sessions with the hairdresser for that "well-set" coiffure so indicative of nobility and face-saving consultations with beauty experts to find just the right program of personal skin care.

For the gentlemen, there were hurried pursuits of some passing fancy, across-town trips to the temple bank to visit their gold ingots and neck-saving consultations with financial advisors to find just the right program of monetary survival.

It was too much! The "good life" was so taxing, so exhausting; midafternoon rest and relaxation were imperative. Hence a change of pace was in order—a leisurely stroll along a shade-cooled garden path, followed by an all too brief "happy hour" under a vine-covered arbor (the flow of red wine bringing maximum muscle relaxation). Having thus shed their tensions and feeling utterly at ease, the played-out loungers could at last wend their way home—for soothing head-to-toe rubs with perfume-rich ointments and rejuvenating catnaps on pillow strewn ivory couches.

Then they arose to dress for the evening's rounds!

And not a moment too soon. For at sunset "The City" stretched herself luxuriously, lit her ornamental boudoir lamps and kaleidoscoped a gaily-colored *Samaria after dark* dream world out of free-spinning baubles, bangles and beads.

It was all there. Morning, noon and night. A perfect environment. A man-made "millennium." A sweet life with only one trifling inconvenience, one annoying "fly in the ointment."

The prophet Amos.

Amos, that rough, tough, backwoods prophet of God with his voiceprint message of woe.

IVORY PALACES

"Gather together on the hill of Samaria, And see the dreadful disorders there, How oppression flourishes in her heart" Amos 3:9, Phillips).

The buildings still rise . . .

The rolling hill country of Ephraim, where Samaria lounged so gracefully, was a natural beauty spot on the map of the ancient world. It was a veritable paradise—its tree-strewn acreage reminiscent of Eden, its idyllic heights suggestive of Shangri-la.

It was also a land developer's dream come true, and promotional material for a choice residential park *could well have read:*

LIVE IN SAMARIA HEIGHTS
A "GOOD LIFE" COMMUNITY
HILLSIDE LIVING AT ITS FINEST
WOODED SITES   OLD OAKS   MOUNTAIN GREENERY
PANORAMIC VIEWS   REFRESHING BREEZES
A FEW BLUE-CHIP PROPERTIES AVAILABLE
FOR TOWN HOUSES
PRESTIGE HOMES   PALATIAL LUXURY ESTATES

LIVE A LIFE APART in a resort-like setting for city dwellers
. . . away from the hustle and bustle of big-city crowds . . .
upwind from urban stress . . . above the masses.

IDEALLY LOCATED in the heart of the highlands . . . not far
from busy trade route intersections . . . freeway-close to
Judea, Bethel, Galilee and Jezreel . . . easy access roads to
major shopping centers, recreational areas and local
temples.

DWELL IN PROSPERITY under your own vine, your own fig
tree . . . like Ahab, plant your own gardens of herbs . . . like
Omri, build your own ivory palace.
ENJOY THE PRIDE OF OWNERSHIP   LIVE LIKE A KING
YOU OWE IT TO YOURSELF

The Great Samaria Dream House was not the rose-covered
cottage of American traditions. It was not the ubiquitous
Southern California bungalow popularized a few decades ago,
or the redwood-sided, shake-roofed model of today. Nor was it
an up-and-coming "Manhattanized" San Francisco tower-
house.
It was a palace. A lush, plush, intricately carved ivory-over-
hewn-stone mansion designed to showcase the brilliant social
affairs of the day. *It was an "ivory palace,"* luxuriously appointed
with the stuff of which museums are made—exquisitely-
wrought ivory figurines, vessels of ivory, and couches, chairs and
cabinets legged with solid ivory supports. *It was a "great house,"*
paneled with elegantly-carved ivory reliefs, walled with ivory inlay plaques embellished with semiprecious stones and gold,
ceilinged with brilliantly-painted vermilion beams and roofed
with garden terraces bounded by ornamental lattice work.

Anything less would have been unthinkable!

Naturally the wealthy Samaritans "owed it to themselves" to live like the kings—not a one of whom was noted for his petty economies.

There was Omri, for example, the founder of Samaria—building his splendid palace on native rock, importing skilled Phoenician artisans with a "cost is no object" freedom of hand. Then there was Ahab, his son, bringing home his own Phoenician import (a blushing bride), adding on to his father's house so lavishly with ivory it became renowned as "the ivory house which he made."

Lastly, there was Jeroboam II, the reigning monarch in the day of Amos—building his own "king's house" on a still higher level, and at the same time constructing vast subterranean storehouses to contain the overflow riches of the land.

This then was Samaria . . .
A model "good life" community of beautiful homes for beautiful people. A city-on-a-hill crowned with impressive monuments and magnificent structures.

A city-capital rooted in the ways of Omri and Ahab, grounded on the hard rock of the Ephraim Dome and raised stone upon stone with technical skill and artistic perfection.

A tower of ivory, finely textured and highly polished, gleaming in the sun. A rising "obelisk" to the Samaritan Dream.

But this also was Samaria . . .
A Capitol Hill potholed by graft and corruption.

A land of unscrupulous slum lords, land seizures and bloodstained land-use studies legalized after the manner of Jezebel's "affair Naboth" in nearby Jezreel.

A complex of stately edifices built on rough stones of covetousness and greed, mortared at the expense of little men caught in the crush and maintained by oppression of the helpless poor.

A city of beautiful homes stashed with the fruit of crime and violence; treasure-filled rooms furnished with guilt-edged possessions and secret storehouses stockpiled with purloined goods.

To this city, as representative of the entire Northern Kingdom of Israel, Amos voiced the warning condemnation notice of God: "The ivory-paneled houses will be destroyed, and the great mansions shall be no more."

BY ORDER OF THE LORD

THE FOREMOST NATION

"Alas for the complacent ones in Zion, Who live on the heights of Samaria without a care, Appointed leaders of the foremost nation, Respected by the whole house of Israel!" (Amos 6:1, Phillips).

> "A mighty fortress is our God, A bulwark never failing . . .
> "Did we in our own strength confide, our striving would be losing . . ." (Martin Luther)

If there had been a "Capital City Beauty Contest" in the days of Amos, Samaria would have won hands-down. Runner-up would surely have been her older sister, Miss Jerusalem. (Under King Uzziah's energetic Southern Kingdom regime she was shaping up nicely.) Other finalists would have been Miss Tyre (Phoenicia), situated north of Samaria's throne; Miss Damascus (Syria), positioned farther north and east; and Miss Gaza (Philistia), off to the southwest.

Left in the wings (because of internal disorders), would have been Miss Ashur, the ailing titular capital of Mesopotamian Assyria, and Miss Ninevah, her alternate.

"Miss Capital City" "Miss Middle East" "Miss Ancient World"

So it would have gone. Without a doubt, bright-eyed, ivory-skinned Miss Samaria would have captured every available title. As anyone could see, she was more than just a pretty face—she had youth, personality, brains and vital statistics that evoked admiring "oh's and ah's" from even her competitors.

For one thing, she was built along statuesque lines. Strategically founded on a three-hundred-foot hilltop that rose in solitary splendor above the local plains and valleys, she towered head and shoulders over her surroundings. Fortressed by King Omri, further strengthened by Ahab his son and refortified by Jeroboam II, she was every cubit a sight to behold.

Her measurements were staggering. From head to toe huge walls of well-dressed limestone blocks (laid in courses of alternating stretchers and headers) increased her natural dimensions. On her level summit an encircling band of parallel inner and outer walls double-crowned her stately brow. Along her banked slopes solid stone-to-stone walls twenty, thirty, even as much as thirty-three feet thick girdled her ample sides. At her feet (near her northern city gates) a massive one-hundred-eighteen by fifty-three foot bastion broadened her already widespread base.

Never was fair lady so generously endowed!

More than a natural beauty, more than a natural stronghold, Samaria was a mighty fortress. In addition to being able to support herself indefinitely (with wall-safe fields and vineyards, a hillside spring and numerous rock-dug cisterns), she was also skilled in the art of self-defense.

Not without reason was she called "the Watch Hill." From her uppermost reaches a single watchman commanded a sweeping view of enemy approaches. From her ramparts unerring archers picked off hostile troops attempting to maneuver the rough-tracked land below. From her hilly fastness well-trained armies emerged to defend her national integrity with a show of strength.

And rightly so! There were "wars and rumors of wars." Military preparedness was the divine order of the day. Proper defense against enemy attack was absolutely imperative to her well-being.

Jeroboam II was not deceived.
It was not Samaria's contoured hills but firm military lines that commanded respectful "oh's and ah's" from other nations.
It was not wide-eyed naivete but military alertness that discouraged improper advances from foreign powers.

Accordingly, Miss Samaria ruled her world with a firm hand. Under the brilliant military leadership of Jeroboam II, she lost no ground but pushed out beyond her local boundaries, out beyond the sometimes limits of Dan on the north, the river Jordan on the East. Damascus was hers, long-lost territories of Transjordan were recovered, Gilead and Bashan again annexed to her borders.

In alliance with Uzziah of Judah (famed for his strongholds, defensive towers and inventive missile system), she changed the map of the Middle East. Indeed, as the prophet Jonah foretold, Jeroboam II "restored the border of Israel from the entrance of Hamath as far as the sea of the Arabah (the Dead Sea)."

Nor was this all. For years Samaria-Israel reigned from her hillside throne as absolute monarch over a vast Fertile Crescent domain: collecting prize money from tribute-paying lands, controlling East-West communication lines, channeling favored nation trade winds along the Trunk Road and conducting foreign affairs from a position of summit strength.

For years lesser nations stayed at a respectful distance, and she enjoyed peace on all sides.

But alas for Miss Samaria . . .

It was right in God's Book that she should take her place among the nations—head held high, beautiful, generously endowed.

It was right that she should secure her borders and defend her honor with something more effective than a hatpin jab.

It was right that she should try out for *"Miss Invincible,"* *"Miss First-Rate Power"* and *"Miss Foremost Nation."*

But it was not right that she should become complacent, settle on her *lees* and fancy herself *"Miss Sufficient Without God."*

Neither was it wise.

NUMBER ONE

"Therefore they shall now be the first of those to go into exile..." (Amos 6:7a RSV).

A young man strives to get ahead . . .

It was the eighth century before Christ, and more than the camels were humping in Israel. From Dan to Beersheba there was a universal struggle to be "Number One." From the pride of Jordan to the tribe of Ephraim, it was "me first" all the way.

Throughout the length and breadth of the land, the law of the jungle prevailed.

In a sense, this was not surprising, for large portions of the land itself were as yet untamed. Long-clawed brown bears, ravening evening wolves, bold leopards, panthers and tigers roamed the pristine forests. The mournful cry of pack-bound jackals on the prowl, the baying of wild dogs in search of carrion, the roar of hungry lions thundering over their helpless prey—these were bone-chilling realities of the day.

Indeed, ancient Palestine was lion country, and along the banks of the Jordan the king of beasts reigned in regal splendor. Lying in wait by day among the tall grasses lining the river's edge, lazily whisking his long tasseled tail, half-closing his sleep-filled eyes; watching, waiting—by night he arose to roam the land in prides, tearing at the throat of his victims with great teeth, killing with a single smashing blow of his paw.

Canaan had always been a rugged land in which to live. Not only had it offered the early settlers of Israel great potential as a land "flowing with milk and honey," it also demanded of them an overcoming spirit. From the first, they struggled to survive.

At the time Israel crossed over Jordan, the Canaanites (as well as the wild beasts) were firmly entrenched in the land. The going was rough everywhere, especially in the hill country assigned the descendents of Ephraim. Joshua's challenge to his brothers was therefore direct and to the point: "The hill country shall be yours, for though it is a forest, you shall clear it and possess it to its farthest borders."

So *clear and possess* Ephraim did. For years the tribe wrestled with the land, with broken terrain, with unfelled trees, with reluctant crops, with extremes of weather and with wild beasts. For years the tribe wrestled with Philistine cattle rustlers, with Canaanite "chariots of iron," with the Perizzites, the Rephaim and the Amorites, whose height was "like the height of the cedars" and whose strength was "as the oaks."

They wrestled and survived. They put down stakes and gained a foothold in the land. They endured hardship and emerged stronger than before. They were courageous, vigorous, enterprising—true pioneer stock.

In time, they expanded their borders. Having already gone west and made their fortune, they looked for new frontiers to conquer. At their side languished the tribe of Manasseh (their brother-tribe from the loins of Joseph). As their forefather Jacob prophesied centuries before, the younger Ephraim soon outdistanced the older Manasseh in every respect: bringing his chalk-poor land under subjection, absorbing his identity as an individual entity and ruling over the "thousands of Manasseh" with the "ten thousands of Ephraim" Moses had forseen.

Over a period of time, the remaining northern tribes of Israel also became one with the mighty Ephraim. As satellite nations, they followed his lead in uniting with Judah under the reign of David. Later, the Ephraimite, Jeroboam I, was their overseer in King Solomon's court. Still later, they revolted with Ephraim at the onset of the ill-fated reign of Solomon's son, Rehoboam.

After the civil break with Judah, Ephraim once again led the way among the tribes. The capable Jeroboam I was immediatley raised up by God as king of the newly-formed Northern Kingdom, and roughly a century and a half later, Jeroboam II (the second Jeroboam), was raised up by God as national deliverer. During his lengthy reign, the northern capital city of Samaria became so powerful, so influential in foreign affairs that it lent its name to the whole land.

By that time, the terms Ephraim, Israel, Jacob, Joseph and Samaria were often used interchangeably, and Samaria itself symbolized the nation of Northern Israel (just as one day Washington, D.C. would symbolize the United States.)

So much for the wild beasts of the land, for the lions of the Jordan pride and for the men of the tribe of Ephraim . . .

By the time Amos arrived on the scene, there was not much to choose between them. Each was Number One in his line— *head of the pack in a bite-and-devour society.*

Amos was appalled. It was not the wild animals of the hills that were endangering the nation; it was the untamed, animal-istic men of Israel. It was not in the leopard-concealing scrub or in the panther-populated bushwood thickets that a man need most fear for his life; it was in beautiful downtown Samaria.

For Samaria was a jungle! A high-rise hand-carved ivory jungle. Within its fortressed walls strangers were not only taken in, they were taken for all they were worth. In its marketplaces bawling animals ran a poor second to vicious, rapacious, cut-throat merchants who mercilessly priced-gouged the poor. On its streets roving packs of wild dogs yielded ground to un-principled men with dog-eat-dog ways; men ruthless in their climb to the top, nipping the heels of their leaders while tram-pling the bodies of their underdogs.

From the bottom of the pile to the top of the heap, from the twolegged "little foxes" with their cunning underground tactics to the social-climbing lounge set with their lion's share of the wealth, there was nothing but power struggles, maneuver-ings, pouncings, fleecings and bloodlettings.

The men of Israel were destroying themselves! The very spirit of aggression that had stood them in such good stead during their pioneer days, that competitive up-the-ladder drive that had forged their nation, had become an overreaching spirit of greed. Materialism had become their god. The love for "Number One," their master.

With a covetousness near kin to idolatry they "cleared and possessed" everything that got in their way. Upward mobility was the one thing that counted. To be at the top of the perch— the Big One, the Executive of the Day, the Man of the Year—was a thing to be grasped whatever the cost. To possess the most ornate great house, to host the most lavish parties, to "keep up with the Jeroboams": these were goals to be reached no matter who paid the price.

Indeed, to pursue and overtake, to have and hold, to garner and stockpile: these were the sum total, the "farthest borders" of their existence—*and all to the exclusion of God.*

Over the years, the tables had turned.

No longer were the men of Ephraim echoing Joshua's "As for me and my house, we will serve the Lord." No longer were the young of the land being encouraged to hunger and thirst after righteousness, to strive for truth, to achieve nobility of soul.

No longer was there caring for the rights of others, compassion for those less fortunate or concern for another man's trembling. No longer was there remembrance, or even knowledge, that in a "nation under God" there could be only one Number One . . . *and that was God Himself.*

Would the men of Ephraim-Israel persist in their rabid "mad dog" ways? Would they be so determined to be Number One they would bite and devour their own kind on their way to the top?

Then they could. God would not violate their free will.

But let them be forewarned. Neither would He continue to prepare before them a table in the presence of their enemies.

One day their banquet would be removed, those who stretched themselves so luxuriously would be confined; another godless nation would move in, take over—and Ephraim-Israel would be first in one thing only, *the first to go.*

"Therefore they shall now be the first of those to go into exile . . ."

THE LIBERATED COWS

"Listen to this charge, you cows of Bashan, Women who glitter on the heights of Samaria . . ." (Amos 4:1, Phillips).

A young woman strives to become "her own person."

Enough of the men of Israel. What of the female of the species? On his brief visit to the Northern Kingdom, Amos took time to find out—indulging along the way in a most perceptive bit of girl-watching (sanctified, of course).

Boldly he lifted his eyes to Samaria's fabled heights. Behind every man was a little woman, pushing hard. Behind every eager-beaver husband was a strong-minded wife, inciting him to action. Scheming, goading, "helping" him onward and upward to bigger and better things. *If the men of Israel were destroying themselves with bite-and-devour greed, how much more their voracious mates!*

As "first ladies" of the land, their wants knew no bounds. Their demands, no limit; their wills, no restraint. With insatiable appetites they downed everything and everyone in their path. The little "indispensables" of gracious living—a prestigious address, an air-cooled summer retreat, ivory-veneered status symbols, jewel-encrusted creature comforts, fatted calves, lambs out of the stall—all were consumed without a backward glance.

What if their "good life" cravings were pressuring their husbands to make a "decent living" by indecent practices? Pushing them into underhanded ways, forcing them to cheat and steal?

What if their own ambitious steps towards self-aggrandizement were running roughshod over the poor of the land? Trampling on the needy, crushing the helpless underfoot?

That was no concern of theirs. They had their own interests.

"Bring us wine to drink."

And bring their husbands did. No Saint Bernard dog in the Swiss Alps ever came to the rescue more readily than the well-trained husbands of Samaria. For all their masculine show of strength in the marketplace, their loud frightening bark on the city streets; at home they "fetched and carried" with unquestioning submission.

At home, they knew their place and kept to it. They came to heel and contented themselves with an old bone, a pat on the head and an occasional reward. After all, they were accustomed to standing quietly in their wives' shadow. (Besides, anything was better than dwelling "with a brawling woman in a wide house.")

Yes, these liberated ladies had come a long way. There was not a born pillow-plumper or "dowdy-housewife-stay-at-home" in the lot. The so-called traditional role of "wife-mother-sexual object" was no more, and the days of "Sarah, put the kettle on" were over.

Gone was the "Yes, my lord" response Sarah offered Abraham from a love-kissed heart, and the virtuous woman of *The Book of Proverbs* (doing her husband good and not evil all the days of her life) was not only more precious than jewels, she was scarcely to be found.

In her place was the NEW WOMAN, the NOW WOMAN,

vocal and articulate about her "rights," shoving to the fore, confronting and confounding, clamoring "I want some freedom to be ME!"

The prophet Amos took a long look around him. The hill country of Ephraim resembled a domestic disaster area, not a peaceful pastoral scene; an invaded lion's den, not a love nest.

The "girls" were everywhere, pretty maids all in a row—taking bigger and bolder strides, throwing their weight around, pushing, prodding, bullying their husbands, stomping, bawling, bossing . . .

Amos paused to ponder. There was something about them that was vaguely reminiscent of his rural background. But what could it be? They could hardly be called little deers or dewy-eyed does. Surely, they were not bunnies, or pussy-cats, or chicks; nor were they the idealized girl of the poet Keat's imagination: "She is like a milk-white lamb that bleats for man's protection."

No. They were none of these. They were more like cows. Not just plain, ordinary, everyday cows, but the pampered, petted, plumped-out bossies from the green grass pasture lands of Bashan.

That was it! They were like the cows of Bashan!

The similarities were inescapable.

The choice breed of cattle grazing the rich grasslands east of the Sea of Galilee were thoroughbreds through and through. *So were the pedigreed kine* that stocked the Samarian hills.

The cows of the Bashan pastures were trouble afoot. Strong, unruly, self-assertive and injurious to all that crossed their path. *So were the heavy-hoofed livestock* at home on the Ephraim range.

The well-fed Bashan cows were of magnificent proportions, renowned far and wide for their heft and girth. *So were the domestic bovines* that exceeded the feed limit at the fancy watering places of Israel.

They were too much, these women! Overbearing, overbred and overstuffed. But there their likeness to the Bashan cows ended.

By no means could they be called "contented."

Just the opposite was true.

Beneath their self-seeking ways was a grass-roots discontent. For all their restless strivings, they were still unfulfilled.

The selfhood they so desperately sought had not come to them with the lowering of barriers and stampede for "rights." The sense of personhood they so yearned for had eluded them, even though they pursued it with unlimited freedom "to be ME."

In spite of the feminine mystique image raised a rough century before by *that most beautiful, talented, brilliant, shrewd, scintillating, fanatical, Number One Women's Liberation Superstar of All Time, Ms. Jezebel*, something had gone wrong.

Something was still missing from their lives.

Amos was sad at heart.

The cattle on a thousand hills belonged to God, but not the "cows of Bashan" glittering on the heights of Samaria. In their eagerness to become their own person, they had gone too far.

Would they persist in their self-appointed ways? Would they continue to lift up their heel against God?

Then they could. God would not violate their free will.

But let them be forewarned. When their men were columned for exile, they would be left unguarded and unprotected from invading enemy troops. They would be women totally on their own at last. Then when they attempted to go their own way, to make a way of escape, they would be overpowered—rounded up as fatted calves for the slaughter.

After the manner of the day, their "rights" would be stripped from them. Their liberties, removed. They would no longer be "wife-mother-sexual objects," but sexual objects only—succulent delicacies to be passed around by men hungry for a taste of Samaria's prime stock.

When the feast was over and they had been consumed without a backward glance, they would no longer be considered sexual objects, but animals only. Hooks would be inserted into their jaws and nostrils; they would be dragged headlong through breaches made in the city walls and herded like cattle to a land not their own.

A land where death would be their only liberation.

GREAT TUMULTS

"Assemble yourselves upon the mountains of Samaria, and see the great tumults within her, and the oppressions in her midst" (Amos 3:9b, RSV).

THE TAX BITE
THE SHOPPING CENTER
THE MAN IN THE STREETS
A DAY IN COURT
OF RIGHTEOUSNESS AND LOVE (SO-CALLED)

THE TAX BITE

". . . the first mowing, which went as taxes to the king" (Amos 7:1c TLB).

The harried American man—wife-supporting, child-raising, home-buying and dog-owning—has more than a passing acquaintance with the high cost of living and the IRS 1040 Income Tax form . . .

The poor men of ancient Israel had a lot with which to contend: the never-ending struggle for Number One status, the care and feeding of the ivory-stalled "cows of Bashan," the cost of maintaining their lounge set lifestyle—and taxes.
All this, and taxes too!

This was nothing new. Actually, the certainty of "death and taxes" had been well established centuries before. The royal right of kings to levy taxes on income from flocks and produce was summarily enforced in all the early Canaanite kingdoms, and the cruel practice of flogging tax evaders with sharply barbed whips known as "scorpions" was all too common throughout the ancient East.

Unfortunately, the average man, caught in such a painful tax-crunch, could only hope to escape the dreaded tax blow by death or by the occasional exemption granted for exceptional military service. But since this rare reward required the type of courage David exhibited before Goliath, not too many men qualified for it.

Now in the days when Israel first settled the land, civil government (as ordained by God through Moses) was a relatively simple thing. It was instituted for the good of the people and designed to function on their behalf.

The levying and collecting of taxes was likewise relatively simple. As outlined by Moses, the tax schedule was structured to be not only equitable, but limited as well. There were to be no additional taxes, no hidden taxes. No tax on tax.

Perhaps it was too simple! Possibly the children of Israel felt they were missing something by not being heavily taxed as were their more worldly neighbors. In any event, when they petitioned God for a king, they were explicitly warned of the dangers ahead—including the obvious pitfall of excessive taxation. Nevertheless, they persisted. "No! but we will have a king over us, that we also may be like all the nations . . ."

Eventually, they had their way, and Israel was never the same again. For with the advent of the kingly rule came a big government, a big name and a big tax bite—"the king's mowing."

"The king's mowing." Never was a term more apt. Under the kings, the tax bite cut deeply into the income of the people. Under the kings, limited taxation was relegated to the past; multiple taxation was the order of the day.

The first seed, the first growth, the first crop, the first "mowing," the first fruits, the first flocks—all were by sovereign rights the property of the king (and of the king's men).

Nothing was left untouched. Like a reaper wielding his sickle in a grain-laden field, the government moved throughout the land with free-swinging strokes—clipping, shearing, lopping, slicing from the top everything that was of value.

Soon there was little a man could call his own. Least of all,

23

his soul. King Solomon saw to that. Not content with tribute monies exacted from subject lands, import duties imposed on foreign caravans and spice-rich gifts *a la Queen of Sheba*— spendthrift Solomon taxed his own people to within an inch of their lives. Some were pressed into bankruptcy; others, into forced labor. And all groaned under the tyrannical rule of taxes, taxes and more taxes.

But the worst was yet to come! Solomon's son, Rehoboam, threatened to reinforce his father's tax yoke with the boast: "I will chastise you with scorpions." The kingdom split in two. The Ephraim tribes (bent on Number Oneness in any case) stoned the tax collector, pulled up stakes and relocated themselves to the north—with their own big government, their own name and their own "king's mowing."

After that, there was no end to the fiscal bite!

King Jeroboam I increased the tax load to support his state sponsored "sacred cows." Kings Nadab, Baasha, Elah, Zimri and Tibni maintained it to support themselves.

Master-builder Omri taxed oppressively to get Samaria off the ground; while luxury-loving Ahab imported eight hundred and fifty Phoenician prophets and enjoyed a summer ivory-white house at Jezreel—all at public expense.

Nor was that all. In subsequent periods of adversity (when tribute money flowed out of the land), Kings Ahaziah, Jehoram, Jehu and Jehoahaz taxed all but the imagination. And in times of prosperity (when corruption in government overflowed all bounds), Kings Jehoash and Jeroboam II taxed *even that!*

The poor men of Israel! All those taxes and not even a toll-free number to call for IRS assistance!

THE SHOPPING CENTER

"Listen, you merchants who rob the poor ... using your weighted scales and under-sized measures . . . selling them your moldy wheat . . ." (Amos 8:4a, 5b, 6c, TLB).

In the slum area of a major West Coast city, a market-shopping housewife, pushed to the wall by inferior products, short-weighted items, moldy bread and tumble bins of "fiction bargains," vainly tries to exercise her boycott muscles . . .

Across the tracks, a fledgling man about town is ruthlessly victimized by "bait and switch" advertising, an odometer adjustment and an "easy term" contract with exorbitant processing fees . . .

Up the street, a prestige gift shop offers so-called "priceless treasures" with double-priced tags affixed; down the street, a cluttered garage pushes substandard parts and runaway repairs . . .
At the house on the corner, a racketeering door-to-door salesman shows an elderly lady where to sign. "Such a nice young man . . ."

Meanwhile, back at the shopping center . . .

The cosmopolitan shopping centers of Samaria were grand and glorious affairs. Instead of covered malls and close-cropped walls, they offered open spaces and expansive skies. In lieu of air conditioning, fluorescent lighting and programmed background music; they promoted natural air, direct sunlight and the harsh all-out sounds of an Eastern bazaar. In place of neatly stacked, racked and departmentalized merchandise; they overflowed helter-skelter stocks of hard goods, soft goods, foodstuffs, cattle, fashions, homespuns, foreign imports, treasures and schlock.

There was something for everyone!
For the local bevy of middle-aged housewives, there were "made in Israel" fashion labels, brownish-red pottery rouge pots, bittersweet pomegranate wines and amulets with magic inscriptions.
For the effeminate males (bent on achieving the popular virile-feminine look of the day), there were flowing robes, subtle fragrances and fine oils to soothe and supple the skin.
For the *nouveau riche*, there were small bronze looking-glasses for personal viewing and large oval basins for celebrity foot washings. For those who already had everything, there were the ultimate in "little nothings"—hand-size gold teraphim (household gods) for private worship and devotions.

The internationally minded were no less favored.
With the military push of Jeroboam II, every door of trade throughout the Middle East swung open, and the marketplaces of Samaria were inundated with foreign-made goods.

From the northern fountainhead of the Great Trunk Road, shipments of brilliantly-colored garments from Assyria and high fashion oasis wear from Damascus crossed the Jordan River at the Bridge of Jacob's Daughters, then joined wine-laden Lebanese caravans at Hazor to flow down through Galilee, the Valley of the Robbers and on to Samaria.

Not to be outdone, the southern branch of the busy Fertile Crescent commerce-way vied for a share in Samaria's till. Up from the Nile streamed "secret" beauty potions, brightly hued nail varnish and kohl from Egypt's shadowed lids. At Gaza, great caravans merged to follow the Mediterranean seacoast northward to the pass at Megiddo, where collector's items from Israel's past (gold-beaded jewelry from the Canaanite-Joshua period, and ninth-century metallic lamp stands) were tagged for Samaria's antique shops.

Near Jezreel, the southbound tributary road from Phoenicia, the Via Maris (the Way of the Sea), joined with the Trunk Road to flood the Samaria market with seagoing goods from as far away as Tarshish (in southern Spain).

Even this was not all!

From the Arabian Peninsula, the Persian Gulf and the East Indies, soft-footed camels shuffled the dusty Incense Routes: Samaria-bound with fragrant powders, myrrh, cinnamon, aloes; exotic perfumes, aromatic plants for medicines, jet-black ebony *objets d'art*, pearls and ornamental peafowls—magnificent strutting birds whose raucous cries and brilliantly-marked trains were only eclipsed by the shrill sounds and flamboyant decor of the marketplaces themselves.

Unfortunately, there was one flaw, one perfection lacking, one commodity out of stock in the cosmopolitan shopping centers of Samaria: fair dealing. *Old-fashioned, honest, open-and-above-board fair dealing was not to be found.* Anywhere. At any price.

It was not only in short supply. It was nonexistent!

Somewhere along the line, Israel had departed from the straight and narrow way. The ancient standard of Hebrew weights and measures kept in the tabernacle was destroyed; the exact copies kept in the households of the people were mislaid.

Not surprisingly, business ethics were also lost in the shuffle.

And although upright kings like David authorized standard weights and measures, by the time Amos came to the Northern Kingdom, it was every man for himself.

Every man was his own yardstick, and his own "king's weight."

It was *caveat emptor* all the way. "Let the buyer beware . . ." especially in the grand and glorious shopping centers of Samaria.

Let the buyer beware of the heavy thumb, the educated finger and the shifting hand.

Let the buyer beware of the double weights (one for buying, the other for selling) and the ephah of wheat "puffed" with animal feed grains.

Let the buyer beware of hand-rubbing proprietors, fast-talking salesmen, "I can get it for you wholesale" wheeler-dealers, "friendly" moneylenders and slick loan sharks.

Let the buyer beware of sharp money deals, blank sales contracts, hidden clauses and the dotted line.

To a man, the dishonest merchants of Samaria were bringing the nation to ruin!

Like the young Jacob, they were swindlers in thought and deed. Like Esau, his brother, they lived only for what was in the pot, selling their noble birthright for "a mess of pottage."

And like many a man confronted with the error of his ways, they were without a redeeming feature—for they admitted no wrongdoing but congratulated themselves on their wealth, took the proud stance of the imposing monuments that crowned Samaria's fair brow and with a single voice proclaimed their most excellent goodness:

"Yet I am become rich, I have found me out substance: in all my labours they shall find none iniquity in me that were sin."

In another place, at another time, the prophet Daniel read the handwriting on the wall for another nation.

"MENE, MENE, TEKEL, UPHARSIN. God hath numbered thy kingdom and finished it. Thou art weighed in the balances and art found wanting . . ."

That nation was not the first to be so weighed and measured by God.

Nor would it be the last.

THE MAN IN THE STREETS

". . . They sell the righteous for silver and the needy for a pair of shoes—They . . . trample the head of the poor into the dust of the earth, and turn aside the way of the afflicted . . ." Amos 2:6b, 7a RSV).

"Rich man, poor man, beggar man, thief . . ."

There he was underneath it all. The average man of Samaria-Israel. The common man, the poor man. The "man in the streets."

In the marketplace, he was a victim; in the tax line, a loser. In the up-the-ladder climb to success, he was lower than low. In the labor force his struggles to get ahead were foredoomed to failure, and in an uncaring society, his attempts to find an identity for himself were senseless and futile.

He was, *and always would be*, a cipher. A nothing.

Like a sheaf of wheat dumped on the threshing floor, the man in the streets was rudely bound, beaten down and trodden underfoot. Like a grain of corn lifted aloft on the winnowing-shovel, he was pitched about, tossed by other men's whims and blown away like chaff.

Like barley crushed between the upper and lower millstones and like a measure of flour brayed by pestle on mortar, he was caught in every crunch, pounded by every pressure, roughed up, ground down, flattened out and consumed.

Nor was he alone. The widow and the fatherless, the weak and the helpless, the afflicted and the infirm, the resident foreigner, the elderly, the innocent—all these shared his plight.

As the "poor of the land," they were destitute of hope. The little they possessed after the high and mighty had their fill was finished off by the moneylender—the local "friend" who approached them on street level with an offer of help.

What "help" he offered! It was not enough that he would charge a poor man exorbitant interest rates, *and* demand all he owned as a pledge, *and* keep his outer garment (his only covering) overnight, *and* break into his house to dispossess, *and* seize his millstone (so his wife would be unable to grind meal to feed his hungry children), *and* force foreclosure on his ancestral property . . .

No! The moneylender wanted blood. Flesh and blood. And by exerting the right amount of economic pressure at the right time, he maneuvered the Great Unwashed onto the dunghill of slavery.

From there the going price of a man was proclaimed:
        FOR THE RIGHTEOUS—A HANDFUL OF SILVER
        FOR THE DESTITUTE—A PAIR OF SHOES

All this was nothing new. From the reign of King Omri on, widespread economic disparities existed in Samaria. By the reign of Jeroboam II, the rich had become so rich, the poor so poor, the lines of demarcation were clearly drawn. It was rich *or poor*, lounge set *or man in the streets*. It was ivory tower *or ghetto hovel*.

On one side were the "haves." The ruling classes, the owners of great estates. The "doctors, lawyers, merchants, chiefs." On the other side, the "have-nots." The underprivileged masses.

One man had everything, and more. The other had nothing but poverty and work, over-the-balcony abuse and downwind stench, ill health and disease, a growling stomach, a fussing child and a wife grown old before her time.

One hand bore rings—the other, scars. And between the two was a widening "no man's land" the rich would not cross over, and the poor could not.

This was not of God.

In the divine order instituted by Moses when the nation began, the commandments: "You shall love your neighbor as yourself . . ." and "You shall open wide your hand to your brother, to the needy and to the poor . . ." were to be carried out in personal and practical ways.

Thus, the law enjoined the wealthy landowner: "When you reap the harvest of your land, you shall not reap your field to its very border, neither shall you gather the gleanings after your harvest. You shall not strip your vineyard bare, neither shall you gather the fallen grapes of your vineyard; you shall leave them for the poor and for the sojourner."

When this injunction was heeded, there was food for everyone. The poor man had opportunity (if he chose to take it) to gather that which was left by the reapers, to feed his family by his own labor and to retain his self-respect while he got back on his feet again.

But in the Northern Kingdom, this could never happen!

Not only were the wealthy refusing to open their hands to the poor: *they were clenching their fists against them.*

Not only were the rich landowners ordering their wheat fields

29

denuded, their olive trees beaten to the uppermost boughs and their vineyards stripped bare (even of fallen fruit); *they were exacting wheat from the poor, and stripping the very robes off their backs.*

Not only were the merchant princes violating every God-given command to decency and honor, and not only were the ruling classes denying basic human rights, *together they were systematically crushing the masses in a wine-press of terror, until the streets of Samaria were vat-splashed with blood!*

A DAY IN COURT

"Let judgment run down as waters, and righteousness as a mighty stream" (Amos 5:24).

A man approaches his long-awaited day in court with mixed emotions. Will it be a day when truth prevails, when right comes to the fore? Will justice take its true course? Or will . . .

The threshing floor at the entrance of the Samaria gate was a place of great national importance: it was there the "guardians of justice" for the Northern Kingdom of Israel gathered.

It was there the king sat upon his judicial throne, surrounded by the lesser lights of the land—the officials of the court, the judges, advocates, witnesses, citizen-jurors and rank and file of the people. It was there the man in the streets exercised his most fundamental civil liberty: the right to a day in court.

It was there the nation Israel had opportunity to divert the impending flow of God's just judgment upon her land by rising up, in *self-examination, self-judgment and self-discipline,* to set her crimes against society aright. And it was there she had opportunity to restore balance to her scale of justice, to redress wrongs and to bring restitution to her oppressed members—*before God Himself must arise to defend their cause.*

Israel's judicial heritage was a proud one: the law of God as given through the man Moses. In every word (from lofty concept to fine print detail, from the spirit of the law to the letter thereof), there was but a single reading: liberty and justice for all.

Under the law, every man stood equal before the judgment bar. King and commoner, rich and poor, landowner and man in the streets. Under the law, every man had the God-given right to be considered innocent until proven guilty, the right to stand trial in open court with evidence introduced through provable testimony in the mouth of two or three witnesses (hearsay being inadmissible), the right to receive an objective, non-biased verdict, and the right to expect the prompt administration of the penalty — or the release demanded by just judgment.

Not surprisingly, the great leaders of Israel respected the law. Moses abided by it. David "reigned over all Israel; executing justice and maintaining the right for all his people." The young Solomon asked God for "an understanding mind to govern thy people, that I may discern between good and evil . . ."

In the Southern Kingdom, Jehoshaphat appointed qualified judges to assume the ultimate responsibility, *to sit in the place of God,* hearing and deciding disputed cases in all the fortified cities of Judah. "Consider what you do, for you judge not for man but for the LORD . . . whenever a case comes to you from your brethren . . . you shall instruct them, that they may not incur guilt before the LORD and wrath may not come upon you and your brethren."

Always, when the nation chose to deal courageously within her courts, God blessed the land.

Sadly enough, this could never be the case in the Northern Kingdom of Israel. There the courts brought down wrath rather than blessing. There the statutes of Omri and Ahab prevailed, not the law of God. There a man could be "judicially murdered" in the courts, as was Naboth the Jezreelite.

Actually, the case of THE STATE VERSUS NABOTH THE JEZREELITE began quite simply. Naboth, the commoner, owned a vineyard inherited from his ancestors. Ahab, the king-judge, coveted it for an herb garden (since it was hard by his summer house in Jezreel). Ahab made Naboth an offer for the property. Naboth promptly rejected it (as was his privilege). "The Lord forbid that I should give you the inheritance of my fathers."

At this point, Judge-King Ahab (feeling vexed and sullen) retired to his chambers. Once there, he laid down on his bed, turned away his face and refused to eat. Thereupon, Jezebel, his loving wife, counseled: "Do you now govern Israel? Arise and eat bread and let your heart be cheerful; I will give you the vineyard of Naboth the Jezreelite!" And give it she did—over Naboth's dead body.

With fanatical adherence to the form of the law, she contacted

31

the court officials (in writing and using Ahab's seal of office). Through them she arranged to have a fast proclaimed, Naboth hauled to open court, two false witnesses set up against him and a charge of treason brought: "You have cursed God and the king!"

With this, Naboth's day in court (and life on earth) ended. He was immediately dragged outside the city and stoned to death. Thereupon, ever-loving Jezebel reported back to Ahab; Ahab gathered his judicial robes about him, came out of chambers— and went out to the garden to plant herbs.

From this, and other landmark decisions by the lethal partner-ship of *Jezebel & Ahab*, Israel learned many things.

She learned the law was good—for covering a multitude of sins. It was useful—for achieving her own ends with impunity.

She learned she could do anything, as long as she did it *legally*. "The form of justice must be done." She could strong-arm the little businessman, *legally*; she could thresh the man in the streets, *legally*; she could dispossess the poor, *legally*; she could condemn the innocent and acquit the guilty, *legally*. She could even kill the spirit of the law—*as long as she kept the letter intact*.

She learned the investment value of a bribe, the inestimable worth of a well-placed "gift." She learned to prize a "smart lawyer," a perjured witness and a corrupt judge. She learned to turn her courts into a legalistic circus by performing side-show antics, twisting justice, rigging trials and walking a fine legal tightrope.

And if anyone challenged her, if anyone dealt courageously with her, he was held in contempt, *legally*. "They hate him who reproves in the gate, and they abhor him who speaks the truth."

For decades, Israel practiced law with a will. For generations she devoted herself to "trials" only remotely concerned with guilt and innocence. Invariably righteousness was cast down, justice took a beating and truth fell in the streets.

Gradually the courts once paved with promise eroded. The cutting edge of the law dulled. Freedoms were given away, rights whittled. Objectivity in law was forgotten; respect for the judi-cial system gone. Lawlessness increased. Calculated violations multiplied. Lawsuits sprang up "like poisonous weeds in the furrows of the fields." Eventually the courts congested, the system backed up. Gall and wormwood-like poisons spewed bitterness over the land.

The threshing floor at the Samaria gate, *the very place* where Israel had opportunity to cure her social ills, became her most noxious offense!

What would purge Israel's judicial system?

What would cleanse the bloodstained threshing floor and loosen the residual guilt that lay like silt atop the court's uneven judgments? What would dislodge the mired tangle of legal gobbledegook, ambiguous readings and subjective interpretations that obstructed the course of justice?

Only a God-given stream of righteousness welling up in the hearts of men, flooding the length and breadth of the courts, opening the door to truth, lifting justice back on its feet, cleansing, purifying and bringing healing to the souls of men.

What would sweep away the logjammed evils, the piled-up sins that hindered the free flow of God's blessing upon the land?

Only a torrent of righteous judgments mounting up with flash-flood urgency to spill liberty and justice over the banks of the courts and onto the low-lying areas of the land.

It was not too late! Israel could still turn wrath to blessing! Amos was still voicing the court challenge of God:

"Let judgment run down as waters, and righteousness as a mighty stream!"

OF RIGHTEOUSNESS AND LOVE (SO-CALLED)

"Let justice roll down like waters, and righteousness like an ever-flowing stream" (Amos 5:24, RSV).

> *Love, love, love . . .*

Never was Israel so awash with love as the day Amos came to town. From border to border, there was nothing but love (so-called).

In the marketplace, love for the Golden Ingot crowded out honesty and fair dealing. In the courts, love for expediency reshaped the way of truth. In the streets, love for Number One took over.

In the temple, a man and his father shared the same love-cult prostitute. On every high hill and under every green tree, love lusted unrestrained. At the feet of the pillared idol-goddess Asherah, as many perversions flowered as petals on the love lily affixed to her hand.

For love of Baal, the young were sacrificed. For love of power, the poor were oppressed. For love of ease, the "cows of Bashan" ran roughshod over the helpless. For love of peace, their weak "bulls" looked the other way. For love of foreign affairs, the whole nation bedded down with a succession of compromising "hired lovers."

Over the years, none of Israel's kings excelled in the field of love as did Ahab (Jezebel's Prince Charming).

In addition to his celebrated flower-picking, herb-planting love (THE CASE OF THE STATE VERSUS NABOTH THE JEZREEL-ITE), the king evidenced an abiding love for all things international (cultural exchanges, ecumenical love-ins, joint economic ventures, treaties, covenants, etc.).

Perhaps the most noteworthy example of this abounding love of Ahab's came at the conclusion of the Seven Day War between Syria and Israel. It was spring, and the sap was flowing; Ahab had just emerged victorious from a pitched battle during which the Syrian troops were all but annihilated, and the Syrian king, Ben-hadad, had been forced to run for cover.

But all was not lost (for Ben-hadad at least). Knowing Ahab's loving nature and his reputation as a merciful king, he sent a dovish message to the naive and gullible Ahab.

"Pray, let me live," he cooed.

"Does he still live?" asked Ahab. "He is my brother."

With that the war was over!

Spurning the revealed will of God, Ahab magnanimously sent for his erstwhile foe, invited him into his chariot, gave him the red carpet treatment and set up a conference table right then and there. So tender was his love, so endearing his compassions, he even allowed his defeated enemy to dictate the terms of peace. Then he made a covenant with him and let him go.

With an open-armed display of "brotherly love," Ahab comforted his enemy and cold-shouldered his own people, joined hands with the sworn enemies of God and betrayed the fighting men who purchased Israel's freedom at the cost of blood.

With a single loving embrace, he sold his country up the river Abana, bought the scheming Ben-hadad time to regroup forces for a future attack and brought down the wrath of God.

Once again God was outraged by this man who "sold himself to do what was evil in the sight of the LORD." This man who loved the evil and hated the good, who loved wickedness and hated righteousness.

This "loving" man with his "holier than Thou" attitude, who deemed himself more merciful than God, more just, more loving . . .

But with this very man Israel was entranced!

With open arms, she enfolded him to her heart. His ways became her ways, his loves, her loves. He was her model, her pacesetter and her national hero—all in one. He was her Brother of Brothers, Great Humanitarian and Lover of Mankind. (It was just prophets he couldn't stand.)

For years his statutes were kept. For decades his following grew. For generations his "loving influence" permeated the land, until, by Jeroboam II's day, the whole lump was so leavened by Ahab's loves (so-called), Israel was a "nation under God" in name only.

Throughout the length and breadth of the land, "love" was not only the last word, it was the only word.

"Righteousness" was not known.

Like a Middle East well, Israel gushed the old oil. Like the old Lake Huleh marshland, she oozed a reeking swamp of putrefying sweetness. And like the landlocked Dead Sea, she stagnated in her own wastes . . . for righteousness had long since evaporated, and a low-lying love was all she had left.

This was unfortunate, for "righteousness exalts a nation . . ." not love (so-called).

DREAM WORLD

"You push away all thought of punishment awaiting you . . ."
(Amos 6:3a, TLB).

DREAM WORLD
IDLE SONGS
THE HAPPY HOUR
ABOVE THE HEAVENS
MUCH ADO ABOUT "NOTHINGS"

DREAM WORLD

"Ye that put far away the evil day, and cause the seat of violence to come near" (Amos 6:3).

Quite by accident, a plump young woman catches sight of herself in a three-way mirror. She is appalled by what she sees—front view, side view and rear view all at once! It is too much.

Obviously, something must be done. Either she must change her ways (diet, exercise, etc.), or she must turn her mirrors to the wall. Or . . .

She has it! Leaving the painful image of herself to the mirror, she hauls out her basic dress pattern and gives it a major alteration—slashing here, enlarging there, easing out the seams and changing the darts to accommodate the latest bulge.

She then cuts out a new garment from her altered pattern, sews it up, adds a bit of slenderizing trim and slips it on. It fits like a dream—without stress or strain. She heaves a

sigh of relief. One more reality crisis is over!
She won't have to shape up *after all.*

Ms. Samaria was too much. She had it all. Beauty and brains, symmetry and strength. A figure to match her burgeoning economy, and a list of suitors a mile long.

Furthermore, as "Miss Foremost Nation" she was unbeatable. In spite of the great tumults in her midst, the widening gap between rich and poor, the oppressions and injustices, she was still Samaria the Beautiful. She was still luxuriously at ease.

Her life screened like a 1930 (A.D.) film. *Sophistication and fantasy plus.* She dined on escapist fare, reveled in conversational fluff and fashioned a dream world all her own. She admitted to no pressing problems, no complex issues and no unsolvable difficulties—at least none that could not be resolved by the last reel.

How did she do it?
How did she wend her way through blood-spattered streets and then trip the light fantastic—without missing a step? How did she cope with weighty problems and face the reality of estrangement from God—without evidencing stress or strain?
She did it with ease.

If she accidentally caught sight of herself in a reality-mirror and saw how badly out of shape she was getting—she averted her gaze and walked on without a backward glance.

If she was caught in a tight squeeze, or if she discovered a widespread problem in her midst—she just let it spread, threw out the established order and adopted a more liberal cut.

If the basic patterns God designed for living proved a bit too restrictive, His "thou shalt not" seam lines too confining, too inhibiting—she expanded them a little, tailored their dimensions to suit her hang-loose ways, scissored as needed and came up with a whole new wardrobe of alternate lifestyles.

If the puritan ethic her forefathers espoused seemed too narrow and strait-laced for comfort, if the inner tension of her elastic morals brought up-tight feelings of distress and guilt—she just eased out her conscience to allow an "everybody does it" leeway, shed her middle-class hang-ups on the couch and discarded her old-fashioned virtues under every green tree.

It always worked!

39

Even when the reality bind was deep-seated, all she had to do was change her patterns—*not herself*—and she felt no stress or strain.

What if she didn't measure up to God's basic black and white, straight-down-the-line rigidly righteous standards?

That bothered her not one whit. Any time she pleased, she could whip up a filthy-rag righteousness of her own, accommodate her ethics to fit any situation, toss on a colorful Jezebel signature-print scarf, restring her Ahab love beads and bat those great big eyes.

What if the truth revealed her faults? No matter. She could always give it a personal bias, stretch it to fit her rationale, trim it with loopholes and embroider it with lies. Then she could cover it with a veil of illusion—and nobody would be the wiser (most of all herself).

What if reality were gaining on her in spite of her best measures? What if she found it harder each day to cope with her outsized problems? Even that was not too much. She could always pull the wool over her eyes, sedate her senses and space out a world of make believe—a dream world of soft lights and sweet music, beautiful people and good life affairs; a paradise unspoiled by reality, untouched by stress and strain; a never-never land with no tomorrow . . .

What if she were inching toward disaster? What if the day of reckoning caught up with her and she had no alternative but to face the "shape up or ship out" message mirrored by the prophets?

God forbid.

"Come, let us eat, drink and be merry . . ."

IDLE SONGS

"You sing idle songs to the sound of the harp, and fancy yourselves to be as great musicians as King David was" (Amos 6:5, TLB).

Music fills the air . . .

Ms. Samaria had it all. Soft lights and sweet music. Good life background sets and sophisticated escapist scripts. Beautiful people with on-camera flare and gala spectaculars with "she shall have music wherever she goes" sound effects.

Because Ms. Samaria lived in a pre-Hollywood musical era, it should not be assumed she starred in silent features. Not at all. Every moment of her day was set to music.

In the best of the old Hollywood tradition, her life unreeled like an all-stops-out musical extravaganza, with lavish out-of-this-world scenery backdropping a fantasia of sight and sound. In her garden party scenes, strolling musicians improvised flowery ditties for easy listening pleasure, in her evening-on-the-roof sequences, light-fingered harpists plucked June-moon tunes. In her candlelight-and-wine seduction scenes, ladies of pleasure strummed up business with songs on the guitar, and in her sex orgy production numbers, the entire cast onstaged for a hair-raising blowout to the sound of flute and pipe.

Actually, had Ms. Samaria cared to do so, she could have scored the story of her life a number of ways, for a wealth of musical literature was at her fingertips. Surely the Great Classics of the Past were available: the Red Sea Cantata by Moses, the Paean of Victory by Miriam and Hannah's magnificent Song of Praise.

The musical works of David, that great poet-songwriter-singer-instrumentalist, were surely at her disposal as well, for David ever filled the measure of his days with notes of purest grace—from reflective psalms imaging the loveliness of his Shepherd-Lord, through gentled songs to soothe Saul's savage breast, on to mighty trumpet-sounding, cymbal-clashing, string-harp-lute-pipe-timbrel-and-full-chorus hallelujahs to the King of kings and Lord of lords.

Or, if "An Evening with David, the Sweet Psalmist of Israel," held no appeal for her, still other musical packages were within reach: "A Sing-Along with Asaph," Elijah's "'Neath the Shade of the Old Juniper Tree" and Jonah's "Great Fish Blues," to name a few.

But none of these "Oldies but Goodies" received Ms. Samaria's nod. Her ears were attuned to a different sound. So, like every generation before or since her day, she took a hand in personally scoring the tempo of her times. Her song stylists fashioned their own trend-setting musical styles, her folk artists wrote their own material, and her tunesmiths hammered out their own art form.

And what did they come up with? What did they dream up as

background music for her "Jeroboam II Fantasy Years" sequence?

A synchronized sound score of *idle songs*—audio confections fluffed with vaporescent melodies, get-away-from-it-all lyrics and cotton candy schmaltz.

Out of lighter-than-air phonic fluff, she fashioned a solid-state dream world—where the cries of her oppressed were muffled with an upbeat doodle-de-do, and the still small voice of the Spirit of God was quenched with a never-ending la-de-da.

If Ms. Samaria could do so much with so little . . . .

What could she have done with such audio aids as stereophonic sound, electronic gadgetry, sophisticated amplification systems, high-precision speakers, way-out tweeters and woofers, instant-play tuners, long-playing discs, endless spool cartridge tapes, high fidelity earphones, private-listening pillow speakers . . .

Hold-in-the-hand transistor radios, round-the-clock disc-jockey broadcasts, piped in middle-of-the-road (M-O-R) background music, computer-controlled barrages of sound in offices, shops and factories . . .

What cries could she have voiced over with the yump-to-yump of guitar-toting young men with beards, down-home country-and-western entertainers with straw-bonnet twang, sophisticated jazz-rock-blues artists, bop-soul stylists, high energy bands . . .

High-voltage rock, theatrical-rock, folk-rock, good-time rock, soft-rock, hard-rock, punk-rock, pop-rock, Bach-rock (as in Johann Sebastian) . . .

THE HAPPY HOUR

"You who drink wine by the bowl-full . . ." (Amos 6:6a, Phillips).

Who is the "problem drinker?"

Is he the skid row habitue holed up outside a run-down flophouse or the prison inmate furtively guarding his fermented "pruno"? The chronic drunk who cannot function without his liquid crutch or the government leader who flies high—even without benefit of a champagne flight?

Is he the high-ranking armed forces officer who hits the bottle regularly or the young serviceman with his high rate of binge drinking? Is he the pressured executive, the "I'll drink to that!" hail-fellow well met or the ego-deflated family man shoring up his masculine image?

Or is he a she? Is the "problem drinker" the alcoholic wife, the secret "9 to 3" school hour drinker, the "empty nest" mother, the lonely widow, or the gray-haired grandmother with unexplained "nervousness"?

Then again, is America's greatest "problem drinker" the teen, the pre-teen or the child alcoholic?

The wines of Israel were great beyond compare. *Par excellence!* as say the French. In any man's language, on any man's tongue, a mere dollop from the sun-blessed vineyards of the ancient land gave transport to bacchanalian bliss.

Indeed, the average man of Israel need not go far afield to enrapture his enological soul. For if he lived in Samaria proper (especially if he owned his own Samaria Heights estate), he could sit under his own vine, peel his own grape and press his own home wine-making kit into service any time he so desired.

And if his abode were in the outer environs of Samaria—the flower-strewn Valley of Jezreel, the swelling hills of Ephraim or the lush countryside beyond—he was already dwelling in a dream world to end all dream worlds.

His was a wine connoisseur's paradise.

One might well imagine a travel blurb of the day:
HAPPY HOUR TOURS PRESENTS
A WINE TOUR OF ISRAEL

IN JEZREEL visit the traditional site of Naboth's vineyard . . . see the ancient wine press cut into the rock . . . watch the barefoot, juice-splashed grape treaders crush the smooth-skinned fruit underfoot . . . enjoy a guided taste-tour of the winery (open 7 days a week) . . .
IN GALILEE inspect the rich olive orchards and dew-drenched vineyards skirting the famed Sea of Galilee . . . run a handful of fertile alluvial basalt soil through your fingers . . . climb a watchtower, leap over a wall . . . meet the more shy-bearing vines . . . (estate labeled wines available upon request) . . .
IN GILEAD stand in awe before the sheltered vines creeping up the westward-facing slopes of the Gilead Dome . . . pay homage to their sweet and delicate grapes, without equal

throughout Israel . . . sniff the bouquet of distinguished wines; treasure the aftertaste of great ones (*you'll get down on your knees to these*) . . .

SIGN UP TODAY

Unfortunately, once Ms. Samaria got down on her knees to the vintage fruit, she couldn't get up again. The cultivated grape proved more cultured, more refined and more mature than she.

For it was not the memory of a haunting refrain that went to her head, nor yet the vision of "dream world" fantasies that sent her reeling—it was the gently staggered hillside terraces encircling her Middle East throne. These were her downfall!

And not hers alone. *All Israel* was as lush as the countryside. *All Israel* bowed low before the varietal fruit.

From the *back street wino,* ferreting out a secluded hole in the wall in which to drink himself into a stupor . . . to the one-rung-up *man in the streets,* keeping himself stoned on cheap wine . . . to the *domesticated male,* augmenting his daily vin ordinaire consumption with weekend binges of the heady beer brewed from local grains . . .

From the lackluster *female of the species,* seeking a lift from her "wife-mother-sexual object" grindstone . . . to the Samaria Heights *grande dame,* as potted as the ornamental palms at her prefeast wine tasting party . . . to the lounge set *bon vivant,* nose deep in a bowl-full of good life wine, spicing the domestic bubbly with bittersweet pomegranate juice, spiking it with the fermented date of the palm. Sniffing, swirling, gurgling . . .

From the *cultish priests,* pouring out libations to the gods . . . to the *rulers of the land,* through strong drink erring in vision and stumbling in judgment . . . to the *king himself,* settled on his lees in an outsized jeroboam . . . *All Israel* was a sodden mess.

"For all tables are full of vomit and filthiness, so that there is no place clean."

In a word, Israel was a nation of drunks. A nation easing into patterns of national disaster and destruction.

A nation spaced out via the vine!

ABOVE THE HEAVENS

"Seek Him who created the Seven Stars and the constellation Orion, who turns darkness into morning, and day into night . . . the Lord, Jehovah, is his name" (Amos 5:8, TLB).

44

Day is done. The circuit-riding sun trails over the western horizon. Night falls. Bright hosts of heaven stud the black-robed sky.

On such a night, a girl makes a wish "upon a star," a young man thinks of "June-moon-spoon" and a child peeks over his shoulder. "The moon is following me!"

On such a night, a woman lingers over her horoscope, seeking "astrological light" for her earthbound way; a man sets up an elaborate system of sensing devices, seeking explanation of recent "UFO sightings"; and a native blames a comet—for making him restless.

On such a night, a young hopeful dreams of spacecraft derring-do; a space agency scientist ponders the latest findings on man's planetary neighbors; and a celestial-snooping astronomer probes the vastness of interstellar space.

On such a night, David lifted his eyes and worshiped. "O LORD our Lord, how excellent is thy name in all the earth! who hast set thy glory above the heavens.

"When I consider thy heavens, the work of thy fingers, the moon and the stars, which thou hast ordained; What is man, that thou art mindful of him? and the son of man, that thou visitest him?"

At the thought of such a God—a God high and lifted up, a God *above the heavens*, a God far above all principality, and power, and might, and dominion, and every name that is named, not only in this world, but also in that which is to come . . . a God invisible and self-existent, a God eternal in Himself, a Creator-Controller-Sustainer-Sovereign God around whom all existence revolves, and in Whom man lives, and moves, and has his being . . .

At the thought of such a God, Ms. Samaria lowered her eyes. Not in reverential awe, nor in humble piety, but in chosen unbelief. She did not like to retain such a God in her knowledge.

Again, Ms. Samaria was not alone. By the day of Amos, all Israel (and much of Judah as well) had joined her in exchanging the truth of God for a lie. In this, they were without excuse.

For although they had no space-age technical knowledge at their disposal and not even so much as a fly-by interplanetary encounter to their credit, the star-spangled skies canopying their Middle East home gave ample witness to the creatorship of God—yet they glorified Him not as God, neither were thankful, but worshiped and served the creation more than the Creator.

After the manner of the heathen, they occupied themselves with the sun, the moon and the "stars" (an oft-used term for lesser-light celestial wonders), and forgot the very God whose glory the heavens declare and whose handiwork the firmament displays.

Professing themselves to be wise, they became fools!

Out of their grab bag of hidden mementos from the Exodus trek, they brought forth personal tote-shrines for their beloved "star gods," Sakkuth and Kaiwan (Moloch, Chiun, Remphan).

Out of their memory-box of the land of Egypt, where temples oriented to the rising sun, and high-rise obelisks spired the morning skies with rays of gold; where the sun, the moon, the stars and the constellations Orion and Sirius were deemed external forms of mighty spirits—they revived an idolatrous love for the heavenly hosts.

Sabaism became the order of the day. Indeed, night and day the "lords and ladies" of the sky were both appeased and adored, as sun-worshipers "put the (tamarisk) branch to their nose" while singing hymns to the rising sun, and devotees of the moon offered crescent-shaped cakes and group sex to their luminous ladylove (hoping to receive, in return, favorable seedtimes and abundant harvests). Even in sophisticated Samaria Heights, roof-terrace home worship centres for burning incense to the Canaanitish and Phoenician cosmic deities sprang up like TV antennas in a suburban community.

No longer was the Word of God honored in Israel. Instead, the lamp to their feet and light to their path was imported from Babylon—where many-storied ziggurats reached for the sky, and many-doctrined priests reached for the minds of men.

It was an age when astrology was in the ascendancy. An age of sky signs, astral influences, ruling planets, celestial happenings; an age of calculating stargazers, monthly weather prognosticators and esteemed priest-astrologer-magicians.

It was an age when the house of man's spirit was empty of divine truth. An age when the superstitious, the naive and the plain bored reached for answers to the riddle of life; an age of exploitation—the blind leading the blind into a ditch.

It was an age of spiritual decline and apostasy. An age when affairs of state were decided by men dependent upon their personal astrologers for insight and leading; an age when the powers of darkness were coming into their own.

"Seek him who created the Seven Stars and the constellation

Orion. . . . The Lord, Jehovah, is His name."

The words of Amos thundered as on a storm-tossed night, illuminating the Eternal God enthroned above the heavens. Yet Israel heard nothing, neither lifted up her eyes.

She was lost in a geocentric world of dreams—where the moon followed her leading, and it dared not rain on her parades.

MUCH ADO ABOUT "NOTHINGS"

"Go on, then, to Bethel, and get on with your sinning . . ." (Amos 4:4a, Phillips).

A man worships at the shrine of the ultimate dream world unreality—a man-made god.

All Israel was religious. From Bethel to Dan, every inhabitant of the Northern Kingdom was deeply involved with the temple, the ritual and the god of his choice.

And what a choice there was! Nowhere but in Israel was there such a stable of gods from which to choose—for when the nation lowered its eyes from the One enthroned above the heavens, the field for man-made, mass-produced gods opened wide. Indeed, the religiosity of Israel was so great, the zeal for ritualistic observance so intense, even the very fields themselves were defiled with idolatrous filth.

Yet it was not to the *altars of shame* in the fields that Amos came, nor the earthy *groves* that symbolized the gods of the starry hosts with crudely carved tree stumps, nor the deeply rooted *centres of Baalism* that spread like devil grass throughout the land (despite Jehu's vigorous hacking). It was not to the *sacred niches* in the rocks at Paneas, nor the *cult centres* Gilead and Gilgal swore by, nor even the *houses of the high places* in the cities of Samaria.

It was to Bethel that Amos came. For at Bethel the most revered god of the Northern Kingdom was in residence. At Bethel the most celebrated of the *golden calves* was stalled.

Now there was more to these golden calves than met the eye.
When Jeroboam I broke with Judah and established Ephraim-Israel as a separate entity, he chose Shechem for his captial seat and royal residence (and Tirzah for his summer home). Thus he provided his people with a place of their own—a *substitute-rival* for Jerusalem, the capital of Judah.

But this was not enough. Although God promised Jeroboam I great blessing if he would lead the newly-formed Northern Kingdom in the ways of the God of Israel, the king was apprehensive. He feared to do so would encourage his subjects to sacrifice in the house of the Lord at Jerusalem, and his hold over them would be lost. "Now the kingdom will turn back to the house of David!"

So he took matters into his own hands. Choosing to disbelieve God's promise, "I will build you a sure house," he deliberately disobeyed. Acting on his own initiative, he put together a *substitute-rival* religious package of his own: the state-sponsored worship of the golden calves at Bethel (twelve miles short of Jerusalem) and at Dan. Thus he broke not only with Judah, but with God and traditional Yahwism as well.

Actually, the "creation" of the golden gods was classic.

In the beginning, Jeroboam I cast off the clearly delineated ways of the living God. The thought of personal relationship with the God above the heavens—the Creator-Controller-Sustainer-Sovereign God around Whom all existence revolves and to Whom all glory is due, left him cold. Such a God would be too much!

So Jeroboam I cast about in his mind for another god. A god he could tailor to his needs. A god over which he could be creator-controller-sustainer-sovereign—a god designed to conform to his image, revolve around him and bring glory to his name.

Not surprisingly, out of bits and pieces of memories racked in the darkened closet of his mind, Jeroboam fashioned just such a god. From impressions gathered in Egypt (where he only recently had enjoyed political asylum during the closing years of Solomon's reign, and where the sacred living bull Apis and the sacred cows Isis and Athor were worshiped), he borrowed the four-footed beast-god concept. Rummaging deeper in the recesses of his mind, he dragged out the golden calf symbol used by Aaron at the Mount Sinai rock festival.

The light went on! Before long, Jeroboam's mental image god was fully conceived and ready to be cast into a media. At that point, craftsmen entered the picture. Molds were designed in conformity to the patterns in the king's mind, molten gold was poured into the molds and in due time, a golden calf came forth.

A god was born!

Success evidently went to Jeroboam's head. Aaron had made one calf; he would make two! One for either end of his kingdom.

The one at northernmost Dan was merely a convenience (a

public service branch worship centre to save travel wear and tear on local religion addicts), but the one at southernmost Bethel was a master stroke of deceit. Only a mind given over to Satan could have devised such a blow to the country.

For unlike Dan (where graven images were well received even in the days of the Judges), Bethel was associated in the minds of the people with worship of the living God. At Bethel, Jacob-Israel, their forefather, made his first vow. Indeed (as Israel's little children learned at mother's knee) Jacob counted Bethel the very gate to heaven, for as he lay dreaming in that place, a ladder of two-way angelic traffic lifted his wondering eyes to the God above.

What better place to *counterfeit worship* of the true God than at Bethel, "the house of God"?

And what better way to *counterfeit spiritual reality* than by taking true ritual and robbing it of meaning?

Jeroboam was a showman, if nothing else. He had no intention of mounting his four-footed follies on bare boards. Nothing short of a theatrical production set in a temple scene would do for his gods. So he "lifted" the meaningful ritual of the Jerusa-lem-based worship of Jehovah—the services, sacrifices and offerings that foreshadowed the Redeemer-King—and rede-signed them to fit his needs. Feasts were retained, but changed in date. Observances were kept, but emptied of meaning. Sacrifices were made, but voided of purpose.

A system of theology was devised, a code of ethics revised. Buildings were raised, standards lowered. A call went out for the role of priests; whoever paid the going price, even the lowest of the people, got into the act. "Something for Everyone" was featured: lust-filled rites, heathenistic hoopla, pizzazz.

To top it all off, Jeroboam I himself, the creator-controller-sustainer-sovereign of the church-state amalgam, the "god of the gods," played lead priest at the opening performance.

"Behold thy gods, O Israel, which brought thee up out of the land of Egypt!"

How could an intelligent people be led astray in this way?
How could a once-godly people so close their eyes to reality that they could no longer discern the gods they worshiped?

True, the golden calves were not put together with American ingenuity and know-how. They were not as impressive as a phalanx of computers, as vast as an industrial empire or as monumental as the rectangular, six-ton block of iron ore altared in the "silent room" of the United Nations building. The rites Jeroboam instituted were not as spectacular as those of a space-age lift-off, nor was his incense burning as breathtaking as a mushroom cloud.

Yet to Israel, the golden calves were not "little tin gods." They were status symbols of the highest order, standing memorials to the nation's heritage as a "nation under God." They were the people's very life—all existence revolved around them. To "kiss the calves," to sacrifice in their honor, to pour out one's life in performance of lavish ritual: these were the end and all of religious experience. The end *and all*.

For these gods were not God, but "no gods." *Idolatry had gone in before the Name went on.* Therefore, they were "nothings." And all that concerned them was merely much ado about "nothings."

With biting satire, Amos sought to shock the people out of their religious dream world and bring them to their senses.

"Go on, then, to Bethel, and get on with your sinning; Go to Gilgal, and pile up your sins. Yes, bring your sacrifices every morning, and pay your tithes every third day; Burn your bread as a thank-offering. Advertise your free-will gifts, be sure everyone hears of them! For this is what you love to do, you children of Israel. . . ."

His words were hard hitting, but they accomplished nothing. *The people had become as empty-headed as their gods!*

WHO CARES?

". . . never a thought do you spare for the terrible miseries of Joseph" (Amos 6:6b, Phillips).

THE SACRIFICE OF FOOLS
DECIBELS RISING
THE DIMINISHED SEVENTH
WHO CARES?
PROPHET SHARING

THE SACRIFICE OF FOOLS

"I hate your show and pretense—your hypocrisy of 'honoring' me with your religious feasts and solemn assemblies" (Amos 5:21, TLB).

A man does his religious thing . . .

Roughly one century and a half elapsed between the reigns of Jeroboam I and Jeroboam II. During that time, many changes took place in the Northern Kingdom of Israel.

The nation's capital seat and royal residence was moved to Samaria; various and sundry kings rose and fell (some with a helpful shove from their immediate successor); the nation itself attained "First and Foremost" prominence atop the Middle East pile.

Bethel changed also. That spot on earth once hallowed by sacred memories of the nation's relationship with God could no longer rightfully be called Beth-*el*, "the house of God." Rather, it had become Beth-*aven*, "the house of nothing." In God's book, it was the epitome of emptiness—the centre of a monolithic religious empire without the living God, its conception vanity, its sacrifices meaningless, its every activity, "much ado about nothing."

A century and a half and the golden calves had not yet attained to deity! They were still the same old "no gods"—empty shells, hollow mockeries without reality, without life and without a redeeming feature.

Then how to account for the calves' great popularity in Israel? How to explain the fact that generation after generation followed Jeroboam I down the cow path of ecumenical expediency?

Obviously it was the easy way to go. Indeed the only way to go as far as the majority of the populace was concerned. Worship of the living God at Jerusalem was forbidden by law; worship of the golden bossies at Bethel and Dan was commanded by law. So . . . .

But that was only part of the picture (and a relatively small part at that). For Bethel was more than Beth-*aven*, "the house of nothing"—it was a *hold of demons*. The original "no god," Satan himself, made sure of that. As the "father of lies," he masterminded the Jeroboam Project from start to finish.

What better place than Bethel to *headquarter demon activity* in the Northern Kingdom? What better place than the king's chapel to infiltrate politics with the Who's Who of Satan's world? And what better way to deceive the nation than through the satanic counterfeit of relationship with God: the media of substitute-rival religion?

"Behold thy gods, O Israel. . ."

From the first, the temples at Bethel and Dan were strongholds against the knowledge of God, and the sacrifices offered upon their altars were offenses against the Person of God.

Yet it was *in the Name of God* the idolators gathered.

In the Name of God, the sincere, the dedicated and the easily duped bowed before the golden altars—drawn by a need to worship, but undiscerning of truth and error. In spiritual blindness, they abased themselves and offered to "God" unseemly acts of devotion. As it was said: "Let the men that sacrifice kiss the calves."

Let living men prostrate themselves before "things of naught

53

. . ." *the breath of their life adoring that which has no breath; the focus of their mind centered upon that which can never think of them; the warmth of their lips caressing that which will never respond . . .*

In the Name of God, the high and mighty thronged the temple services. The wealthy landowners, the merchant princes, the Capitol Hill bigwigs. The lounge set, the beautiful people— every man doing his substitute-rival religious thing in his self-appointed way, for reasons best known to himself.

A man and his father going in to the same temple prostitute, thus profaning the holy Name of God; an estate owner making praiseworthy (and well-advertised) contributions to the temple —with money gained by income tax fraud; a "solid citizen" lounging at the altar on garments illegally seized from the destitute; a "friendly" moneylender drinking wine exacted by unjust fines and extortion; an "upstanding businessman" scheming the next day's balances of deceit . . .

In the Name of God, the self-serving priests capitalized on the people's ignorance. The lowest of men pretending summit talks with God, sending up incense-burning ecclesiastical smoke screens, transmitting theological prattle and gobbledegook.

Priests for hire, prayers for a price. Ravening wolves fattening on the sin-offerings of the fearful; praying mantises eyeing the levels of the temple bank . . .

So it went. Like priests, like people. It was one and the same. Accomplished hypocrites all.

To the God Who can only be worshiped in spirit and in truth . . . the God Who desires mercy and not sacrifice, the knowledge of God more than burnt offerings, obedience rather than the fat of rams . . .

To the God Who hungers for relationship with man . . . the God Who requires a man to walk humbly with Him, to do justly, to hate the evil and love the good, to loose the bands of wickedness, undo heavy burdens and let the oppressed go free . . .

To such a God the religious scene in Israel was a farce, and the sacrifice at Bethel and Dan was the sacrifice of fools.

"I hate your show and pretense—your hypocrisy of 'honoring' me with your religious feasts and solemn assemblies.

"I will not accept your burnt-offerings and thank-offerings.

I will not look at your offerings of peace."

The righteous indignation of God flashed like summer lightning over the spiritually darkened kingdom—yet few souls looked up.

Possibly the worshipers were too busy compiling the *Temple Progress Report* to be disturbed!

DECIBELS RISING

"Let Me have no more of your noisy hymns; My ears are closed to the music of your harps" (Amos 5:23, Phillips).

In the Name of God, *the decibels rise heavenward* . . . . *organists background every moment (from chorale prelude to all-stops-out postlude) with well-timed offertories, prayer-inducing swells and pew-shaking rumbles . . . worshipers sing from well-worn hymnals (hoping stained-glass lyrics will cover a multitude of sins) . . . soloists quiver, vibrate and tremble* . . . .

In the Name of God, *Bach gives way to rock, tradition to more innovative forms . . . agnostics lead believers in a sing-along Messiah (bring your own music) . . . budding young performers loosen up congregations with frenetic rhythms; best-selling superstars showcase their current religious wares with overblown electronic amplifiers . . .*

In the Name of God, *the rafters shake, the heavens are rent* . . .

From the time Jeroboam I staged the first performance of the Jeroboam Follies at Bethel, the traditional music of the sanctuary (as presented in the temple at Jerusalem) was out. The new king had no desire to play second fiddle to the original company, nor had he any intention of playing a game of musical chairs (i.e. "Going to Jerusalem"), and risk finding himself suddenly unseated.

So just as the pure and meaningful worship of Jehovah in ritual and in sacrifice was forbidden in the Northern Kingdom, the pure and meaningful worship of Jehovah in music was outlawed. There was no room in Jeroboam I's religious package for the God-ordained Levitical musicians, the inspired psalms of the faith or the notes of choral praise that echoed the chambers of King Solomon's temple.

Neither was there place for the music in which God delights: the beat of a thankful heart, the melody of a joy-filled soul, the harmony of a mind attuned to the Word of God.

The high fidelity of a faithful worshiper of Jehovah was the last thing in the world Jeroboam I wanted!

So true to his basic substitute-rival pattern, he fashioned a musical package of his own. Out of bits and pieces of audio memorabilia stashed in the darkened recesses of his mind, he taped together a counterfeit song and dance routine that hastened the downfall of the nation.

In the Name of God, the accomplished hypocrites at Bethel and Dan were led to "honor" the Holy One of Israel with a musical score reminiscent of the pagan rites conducted for the Canaanite erotic gods. Thus, the divine Name of Jehovah was retained, the Person of Jehovah disavowed.

Unclean lips sang "His praises"; fingers of iniquity plucked ten-stringed harps for "His glory" . . .

In the Name of God, passion-inflaming decibels soared heavenward—shaking the rafters with riotous singing and un-restrained shouts; raising the temple roof with windy blasts from ram's horns, cornets, flutes, pipes and trumpets loud enough to do a Pharisee proud; rending the heavens with booming ket-tledrums, crashing cymbals, clashing gongs and clanging bells.

Sounding brass jammed the signals of God; noisy hymns masked out the still small voice of the Spirit.

So far as God was concerned, it was too much!

To the One Who listens for music that will invite worship in spirit and in truth, the temple din was intolerable.

Noise pollution at its worst.

In no way was God obligated to subject Himself to such aural abuse! He was not a captive audience, nor a fixed sounding board for hypocrites. The adverse effects of auditory trauma—ringing ears, loss of hearing acuity, irreparable nerve damage, impaired peace of mind, nervousness, tension, fatigue—were not for Him.

So with the divine right inherent in His position as Lord of heaven and earth, He exercised His option to control His aural environment. Without resorting to soundproofing materials, weather stripping, acoustical ceilings or noise-absorbing plastic earmuffs, He solved the temple noise problem by the simple expediency of closing His ears.

"Let Me have no more of your noisy hymns; My ears are closed to the music of your harps."

It probably never occurred to the temple worshipers that God might tune *them* out!

THE DIMINISHED SEVENTH

"You who long for the Sabbath to end and the religious holidays to be over . . ." (Amos 8:5a, TLB).

> *For reasons best known to himself, a man makes his appearance at church. He sits; he stands; he bows his head. He sings; he prays; he reads responsively.*
> *As the sermon begins, he folds his hands, lowers his eyes and smiles beatifically . . .*
> *Inside his head he is out there . . .*

The Sabbath day, as given by God to Moses on Mount Sinai, was to be a sign between the children of Israel and their God. It was to be a perpetual covenant throughout their generations that forever they would remember the Lord Who sanctified them in the wilderness.

It was to be a memorial in time and space: a set-apart seventh of their allotted week of days, when they would set aside the business of living and settle down to love their Maker with their whole being. It was to be a day of refreshment, a day of ease and delight.

A day of mutual enjoyment for man and God.

It was to be a day designed to encourage man *to think*, not act; *to be*, not do. A day structured to enable him to catch his breath, reprogram his thoughts and reorient to the grace of the One Who provided his every blessing—even life itself.

It was to be a day of leisure. A day free from the bondage of work and the shouldering of burdens; free from the stress and strain of travel—the jolts, pressures and hubbub of everyday life.

It was to be a day of rest and gladness. A day without distractions, when a man and his family could unite their hearts to worship the LORD in the beauty of holiness.

Of the same essence were the other "sabbaths" designed by God: the clustered feasts and festivals, the new moons and solemn assemblies, the "holy days" red-lettered on their religious calendar.

So also were the sabbatical years, and the Year of Jubilee— when all work was to be suspended and all joy brought to the LORD.

What a field day Jeroboam I had with all this!

Unlike the Pharisees of Christ's day, who augmented the Sabbath day with way-out legalistic encumbrances, Jeroboam I diminished it—cutting it down to (his) size and lining it up to meet his new lifestyle. Under his updated regime, the God-given "sabbaths" were altered to fit his basic substitute-rival religious pattern, and the observance of the day of rest and gladness became an insult to God.

From the opening day of the temple at Bethel (the fifteenth day of the eighth month, a festival-feast day Jeroboam I devised in his own heart), the people of the Northern Kingdom overflowed the worship services.

In the Name of God, they went through their paces.

They stood; they knelt; they bowed down their heads like bulrushes in a marshy place. They sacrificed; they rejoiced in "much ado"; they kissed the sacred cows; they stretched forth their hands in prayer; they raised the decibel level sky-high . . .

They drew near with their mouths, but their hearts were far from Him. They made the proper sounds, but inside their heads they were *out there* . . .

And what was out there?

The eighth century B.C. forerunner of that twentieth century A.D. great-society phenomenon: THE GREAT AMERICAN WEEKEND.

Out there was the weekly Sabbath freeway exodus, tailgating stock on the trade routes, and the call of smog-free spaces . . .

Out there were such attractions as easy-access roads to local recreation areas, open borders to points beyond, posh lounge-set hideaways, summer houses in the breeze-cooled Ephraim hills . . .

Out there were dune-buggy (camel) caravans leaving for well-watered desert spas, year-round arts and crafts junkets to fabled Damascus bazaars, spring wildflower outings to the Plain of Sharon—where anemones splashed the hillsides with flaming scarlet and white narcissus intoxicated the senses with heady perfume . . .

Out there awaited such kingly diversions as wild animal hunts in the hilly regions of Central Palestine, an occasional Lion Country safari along the wooded banks of the Jordan . . .

Out there was the lure of fresh-water fishing in the Lake of Galilee, spelunking in the rock-strewn caves and caverns around Adullam (David's old haunt), backpacking the Cis-jordan water-parting road . . .

Out there was the world the scheming merchant princes of Samaria longed to return to: the commerical buying and selling, wheeling and dealing world of weighted scales, shorted measures, cutthroat competition and "Let the buyer beware" AFTER SABBATH SALES, JEROBOAM JUBILEE SALES, NEW MOON SIDEWALK SALES . . .

WHO CARES?

". . . but they are not grieved for the affliction of Joseph" (Amos 6:6b).

A man lies wounded by the side of the road—mugged, stripped and left half dead. Another man comes by, sees his plight and passes by on the other side of the road.

The passer-by feels nothing, says nothing and does nothing. Why should he? It is nothing to him, no skin off his back. He couldn't care less.

God couldn't care more for the plight of Israel. In His eyes, this great "nation under God," this illustrious people descended from the proud stock of Joseph, this magnificent "Great Crown Jewel" of the Middle East lay wounded by the side of the Great Trunk Road.

Despite all the golden age prosperity evident during the reign of Jeroboam II (the second Jeroboam), the underlying condition of the nation was grave. Israel was not only being robbed of honor and stripped of godliness, her affliction was going uncared for and unmourned by her own people.

For all its seeming health and vigor in the days of Amos, Israel was a sick nation, a nation in alienation—at once aggressor, victim and "couldn't care less" passer-by.

As a nation, Israel was without natural affection.

In the great houses on the Heights, the beautiful people lounged in an ideal, controlled culture. Like fancy-leaf begonias planted in soil-rich bubble glass containers, they lived a life apart—a "good life" sheltered against exposure to chilling drafts of reality, walled off from close contact with their fellowman and secured by the guarded fastness of their high-rise towers.

It was nothing to them if outside their self-contained units their brothers were subsisting without even the minimum daily requirements for living, falling by the wayside, perishing . . .

What was that to them? They were prize specimens, well cared for—and well able to pass by on the other side of the road.

Not only the affluent few, but the poor alike were without concern for others. The common people were likewise out for what they could get, regardless of the cost to the nation.

The fact that they were destitute dictated their style *but not their conscience*. The bottom rungs of the Number One ladder were no less bloodstained than those at the top; the small-time street thugs were no less deadly than the villainous priests who murdered wayfarers along the Shechem road. The hole-in-the-ground caches of the petty thieves were no less crammed with stolen goods than the vaulted storehouses of the big-time operators.

The "oppressed masses" were not above oppressing—even their own. Moreover, their heads-of-the-house were just as neglectful of their children as the "love everybody" political peacemakers courting oblivion at state affairs.

It was nothing to those "less fortunate" that before God they shared responsibility for the fallen state of the nation—for dragging it down from moral uprightness and plundering it of nobility and greatness, for grinding its once-clean face in the mud and walking away from its misery.

They couldn't care less. They had their own way to make, their own life to live. Their own list of grievances to present.

Of every strata of society, it could be said: ". . . but they are not grieved for the affliction of Joseph."

As a nation, Israel felt nothing and cared for no one, *not even herself*. She was empty headed and empty hearted, as null and void as her "nothing" gods.

Like her cold, lifeless love-objects, she couldn't care more; she couldn't care less. She just couldn't care.

PROPHET SHARING

"Hate the evil, and love the good, and establish judgment in the gate" (Amos 5:15a).

A man lies wounded by the side of the road—mugged, stripped and left half dead. Another man comes by, sees his plight and cares deeply . . .

But what can he do?

One day, Jesus spoke of a man who cared deeply—and knew what to do in just such a situation. Unlike other men who passed by on the far side of the road, this man had compassion on the hapless victim. He knelt at his side, bound up his wounds (pouring on oil and wine) and provided for his care until he was well again.

Unfortunately, the healing of a nation is not that simple. It is another matter altogether. *The solution to national ills is spiritual, not temporal. It is divine, not human.* Apart from God, not even the most well-intentioned "good Samaritan" can raise up, much less restore health to an ailing land.

The Israel to which the prophet Amos came was a land of plenty. A milk-and-honey land of beauty and riches, peace and prosperity, singing and dancing in the streets.
Yet Israel was a land of great tumults as well. A strife-torn land of internal disorder and social breakdown.

Those who labeled themselves "victims of society" sat by the wayside fingering their wounds, shoving aside all sense of personal responsibility as citizens and wedging the "societal breach" with their own brand of prejudice and class hatred.
At the first opportunity, they arose to overthrow the established order. Victims became aggressors; aggressors, victims. It was one and the same. With every attack of violence, the nation took a beating; with every turn of affairs, it staggered and fell back.

The "virgin of Israel" lay fallen on her land. Cast down and forsaken. Prostrate on her own soil with none to raise her up.

"With none to raise her up. . . ."

None save the "remnant of Joseph." None save the believing few, the faithful few who walked in the ways of their forefather Joseph. Entrusted to their care were the spiritual resources needed to bring revival to the fainting land.

In their keeping lay the divine solution to national ills. In their charge lay the future of the nation.

If the "remnant of Joseph" would respond to the message of the prophet Amos in spirit and in truth, fleshing out the voice-print of God with exact word and deed imprints on the sinning land—then the nation might yet live and not die.

If they would loathe evil and love good, set justice on her feet again, and enthrone her in the courts; if, through their example, righteousness and fair play were no longer "meaningless fictions" but everyday realities throughout the land—then the Lord God of hosts would be free to bless "Joseph."

If, through God-directed sharing of the message of the prophets, they could encourage the inhabitants of the land to turn from their wicked ways, cast off their "nothing" gods and return to the Lord their God—then they could expect optimum national recovery.

No power in heaven or on earth could withstand a land that was a "nation under God" in deed and not in word only.
In truth and not in name alone.

Such prophet sharing would not be easy.

To know the message of the prophets, to see its application to the current scene, to be aware of the plight of the troubled land, to care deeply: this would be only the beginning.

To submit personally to the knife-sharp words of the prophets, to be cut to the quick, exposed as a hypocrite, a fraud, to be willing to be humbled and led to repentance: this would require a nobility of soul only God could give.

To work out this inner submission in practical ways, to maintain a "home copy" of right standards (even though government standards might be lost), to retire a heavy thumb in favor of honest business ethics, to correct a tax return, to obey "stupid laws made for stupid people": this would hit close to home.

To break ranks with the uncommitted, to pull clear of the self-defeating victim-aggressor-passer-by cycle, to stand up and be counted, to speak the truth as God sees it, to be righteously indignant in the face of evil—*without apology, without personal animosity or vendetta:* this would demand a wholeness of soul rare among men.

Such prophet sharing would be costly to say the least!

To share the message of the prophets would be to share the occupational hazards of the calling: contempt, reproach and persecution. To be a lone dissenter, a voice "crying in the wilderness," might well bring seasons of despair.

Moreover, if a man faithfully reproduced the voiceprint of God—nothing more, nothing less—if he allowed the divine thrust to place him before those in a position of authority, if he spoke God's truth simply, clearly and honestly—he need not expect to be thanked. For unlike the sugar-coated placebos of the Ahab Brotherhood and the syrupy mouthings of the false prophets, his words would not bring comfort.

On the contrary, they would come as a bitter pill. To the committed backsliders, his message would be harsh and abrasive, not at all the bland coating-action pap an ulcer-prone land would choose. More than that, his diagnosis of the state of the nation would be unacceptable. His warnings of impending danger would seem too doomsdayish; his remedy, "Seek the LORD and live," too simplistic.

Then why *prophet share* at all?

When a man sees the brokenness of his beloved country and that there is "none to raise her up. . . ."
When he cares deeply *and knows what to do*, he does it.

EARLY WARNINGS

"'. . . yet you did not return to me,' says the LORD" (Amos 4:6b, RSV).

SIG-ALERTS
THE HARD WAY
THE BREAD LINE
WATER RIGHTS
FIELDS OF CONTENTION

SIG-ALERTS

"But always, first of all, I warn you through my prophets . . ."
(Amos 3:7, TLB).

The highway patrol posts sig-alerts on a dangerous
stretch of road . . . electronically controlled freeway signs
advise motorists of hazardous driving conditions . . .

Beginning a great distance before a freeway construction
detour curve, unusual flashing lights and attention-getting
signs warn commuters of danger ahead (it is hoped dulled
rush-hour senses will be alerted, and the accident-prone
curve negotiated safely) . . .

The pavement of a quiet thirty-three mile section of
interstate highway is ordered grooved (possibly the tire
vibration and "barroum" noise caused by the rumble strips
will keep drivers from falling asleep at the wheel) . . .

A study is made of the disoriented "wrong-way" freeway
driver—who enters the freeway at an off-ramp, passes
DO NOT ENTER and WRONG WAY signs, goes by a series of

reflecting wedges that shine bright red warnings in the light of his headlights, speeds into the number one lane . . .

On or about 931 B.C., the first divine sig-alert was called in Israel. The place was Bethel; the occasion, the opening performance of the Jeroboam Follies (or Much Ado About "Nothings").

Jeroboam I, the creator-controller-sustainer-sovereign of the golden calves, stood by the temple altar to burn incense. A prophet (known only as "the man of God") suddenly cried out against the altar, "O altar, altar, thus says the LORD: Behold, a son shall be born to the house of David, Josiah by name; and he shall sacrifice upon you the priests of the high places who burn incense upon you, and men's bones shall be burned upon you."

Incensed with rage, Jeroboam I stretched out his hand from the altar, saying, "Lay hold of him!" Immediately, his hand dried up so that he could not draw it back to himself.

Instantly (and understandably) repentant, Jeroboam I sought and received healing from the LORD. He even offered kingly reward and hospitality to the man of God. "Come home with me . . ."

Yet for all his seeming change of mind, *he willfully by-passed the divine warning.* Not only did he refuse to turn from his self-styled substitute-rival religious ways, he increased the cast of priests, thus hastening the nation toward the prophesied dead end.

From that time on, a number of divine alerts were called throughout the Northern Kingdom. For a full century and a half, a succession of God-sent prophets sounded the alarm on the wrong-way nation. *Day and night, they tolled the warning bell.*

Rising up early, "my servants, the prophets" fanned across the highways and byways of apostate Israel. As representatives of the forgotten God (indeed, the soon-to-be-unknown God), they sought to turn the nation from its self-destructive ways.

Stepping out from the ranks of the uncommitted and striding over the fixed line between good and evil, they stood squarely in the path of the onrushing nation. Men of uncommon moral and ethical stature, they lifted high the standards of God. Strong, stalwart uprights, they became "advisory signboards" of divine truth. With short, direct words (designed to catch the eye of a nation on the go), they spelled out the unseen hazards ahead. In no uncertain terms they called good, *good* and evil, *evil.*

The prophets were everywhere. They stood at the juncture of

justice and equality and alerted the nation to the rights of the common man. They rebuked in the gate, crying out against erosion in the courts; they tagged the freewheeling merchants, warning against their double scales and shorted measures. They protested corruption in government, immorality in social relationships. They decried disintegration of national pride.

They were patriots through and through. They loved their land, and cared enough to lay their lives on the line. They loved their land, and entered the mainstream of national life—stemming the tide of evil and holding back satanic forces.

They loved their land, and decade after decade highlighted the way of escape: "Seek the LORD and live . . ."

But Israel would not turn from her collision course. From the first, she would not heed the prophet's call.

Like a "wrong-way" freeway driver, she persisted in her off-ramp religious approach, by-passed every *DO NOT ENTER* warning sign, sped by a series of reflecting lights and veered into the number one lane . . . like a mentally confused motorist on an unknown stretch of highway, she misread attention-getting signs, misinterpreted flashing signals, and became totally disoriented . . .

Like the "hear no evil, see no evil," ivory figurines on her dashboard, she was blind to her plight; with a fine departure from reality, she sideswiped God's truth and mowed down the prophets that spoke it. With windows tightly shut and tape deck yump-to-yumping, she heard no sirens, no alarms . . .

Lost in her private dream world, she ignored the rumble strip vibrations beneath her; blissfully at ease, her senses dulled by food and wine, she nodded and dozed, nodded and dozed . . .

The hour Amos arrived at Bethel, God called a full-scale alert throughout the Northern Kingdom of Israel.

THE HARD WAY

"'I sent among you a pestilence after the manner of Egypt . . . yet you did not return to me,' says the LORD" (Amos 4:10a, RSV).

A man lies flat on his back in a hospital bed. For the first time in his life, he can do nothing to help himself. He cannot sit up. He cannot get up. He cannot even catch a nurse's eye.

Visiting hours are over. The lights are dimmed, the sounds hushed. No longer can he trace the cracks in the ceiling or count the steps in the corridor. Now all he can do is think, and think, and think . . .

God has more than one method of comunication. If a wrong-way nation will not see the signs of the times, slow down and consider where it is headed, if it refuses to heed the "advisory signboards" of the Word of God and learn the easy way: then God will send nonverbal, *hard way warnings* to press the message home. Such was the case with Israel.

Long before the prophet Amos blew the whistle on the Northern Kingdom, the nation was graced with an astounding series of early warnings. Not only were the people given sky-high prophecies to alert them to their true state, they were given *jarring, rumble strip experiences as well.* Pestilence, disease, famine, drought, economic disaster, war: all were sent Israel in an attempt to jolt the nation to it senses, to force a rude awakening *and to cause the people to think, and think, and think . . .*

When the children of Israel were in bondage in Egypt, they were given an "easy way" introduction to the ways of God in sending pestilence, plagues and disease to judge a rebellious people.

In a sense, theirs was a short course. A survey course. They were observers, on-the-scene witnesses to a cataclysmic period in Egyptian history. Cordoned off from the major disaster area, they watched unharmed as God backed His "Let My people go" demands to Pharaoh with a mighty show of ecological strength.

Sheltered by the hand of God and immunized against disease by divine promises, they saw firsthand the effect of the dread-filled plagues on the land. They saw the trembling of the people as the living God challenged the Egyptian substitute-rival nature gods to defend their satanic strongholds. They saw the helplessness of the people as the balance of nature upset on them.

From their sealed-off gallery seats, they watched wide-eyed as one "act of God" succeeded another, as one calamity set the stage for the next. They saw epidemics spawn as the land reeled from the impact of blood-polluted waters, frog sit-ins, sucking insect invasions, swarming botflies, diseased cattle, torturous boils, crop-ruining hail, strip-mining locusts, thick darkness and death.

They saw and learned nothing. For when they later encamped in the wilderness (having been safely ushered out of Egypt by

69

Moses), their abominable behavior triggered plagues that dealt sudden destruction to scores of their own number.

Even when they entered the promised land, they evidenced a learning disability. For though they brought with them *the promise* (if they followed the Lord), "I will put none of the diseases upon you which I put upon the Egyptians," *and the warning* (if they forsook Him), "The LORD will make the pestilence cleave to you . . . and he will bring upon you again all the diseases of Egypt. . . ." they repeatedly botched their record with a long history of heaven-sent pestilence, plagues and disease.

Yet in all this, the mercy of the Lord was great. In all these things, the healing of the land was the redemptive purpose, the peaceable fruit of righteousness the desired goal.

At no time were the divine judgments out of Hand—uncontrolled or uncontained; at all times they were limited in intensity and extent. *Always there was a grace line drawn* beyond which the judgment could not go. Always there was a door of hope open:

"If I shut up heaven that there be no rain, or if I command the locusts to devour the land, or if I send pestilence among my people; if my people, which are called by my name, shall humble themselves, and pray, and seek my face, and turn from their wicked ways; then will I hear from heaven, and will forgive their sin, and will heal their land."

The Northern Kingdom was not without its share of personalized "after the manner of Egypt" judgments. The stroke of leprosy leveled on Jeroboam I at the opening performance of the Jeroboam Follies was only the first of many chastisements. It was swift, sure and labeled by the man of God as a sign of divine displeasure with the advent of nationalized religion in the land. It was limited to the hand of the king; it was removed upon his professed repentance.

But not all "little stroke" judgments sent the wayward people could be so easily identified. The incidence of disease was high in Israel (as in all Near East lands). How much, which or what disease came as judgment of sin would not always be known.

In any case, health hazards abounded in Israel. Venereal disease no doubt plagued the land. Polluted, noxious waters were not unheard of. Malaria exacted a heavy toll. A countryside swamped with low-lying marshlands and overrun with sanitary law violations naturally proved a happy breeding ground for disease-laden insects. Moreover, in the aftermath of sword and famine and in the wake of locust invasions (when the ground lay buried under heaps of rotting corpses), "all these diseases" reached epidemic proportions!

Yet for all this, Israel did not return to the LORD.

THE BREAD LINE

"'I gave you cleanness of teeth in all your cities, and lack of bread in all your places, yet you did not return to me,' says the LORD" (Amos 4:6, RSV).

In social studies class, a young teen slowly shakes his head in disbelief as his teacher speaks of the Great Depression, of "Black Tuesday," joblessness and bread lines. All that happened here?

At the dinner table, he tunes out as his parents discuss cost-of-living rises, escalating inflation, "market basket" reports, lower quality consumer goods, shortages, budget trimming, cutbacks and unemployment spirals. What could his folks know? They're so old they even remember penny post cards!

Only as he comes to the check-out stand at the local supermarket do the economic facts of life press home. Overnight his favorite 2¢ chocolate mints are marked 3¢. Now that hits him where it hurts!

In an essentially agricultural economy such as that of Israel, seedtime-and-harvest fluctuations effect the whole land. If the nation's wheat belt is tightened, every link in the national economy chain alters. If amber-wave grains fail to come to maturity, if fruited plains cast their rich store, all national life suffers.

Moreover, if the "breadbasket upset" condition persists over an extended period of time, the entire nation weakens. The delicate balance of trade with foreign nations ceases to function. The internal economy becomes paralyzed; business falters. Industrial complexes topple, resources fail and economic collapse takes its deadly toll.

From the age of the Patriarchs on, Jewish history was punctuated with periods of severe famine. Periods when everything came to a halt; families were uprooted, and lifestyles changed.

In "good years" of peace and plenty, when the sun coaxed willing crops along and early and latter rains arrived on schedule, when bumper harvests stuffed hungry granaries to the bursting point and wine presses worked overtime—*then the land re-*

sembled a king-sized market basket jammed with bountiful supplies of fresh produce, staples, gourmet foods and wines.

But in "bad years," when rains failed to arrive and drought slowly dehydrated the crops, when insects dined in style while cupboards went bare—*then all Israel lay comatose on her land,* stretched out in flat-on-the-back helplessness.

Not surprisingly, the Northern Kingdom suffered extended periods of economic depression and famine, when cleanness of teeth was involuntary, and lack of bread was a fact of life.

At such times, the sound most noised abroad was not that of grain being pounded into flour on stone mills, but the incessant rumbling of empty stomachs. "Rich man, poor man, beggar man, thief. . . ." Hunger was no respecter of persons. "Doctor, lawyer, merchant, chief. . . ." From the bottom to the top of the Number One ladder, every man suffered want.

There was lack of bread "in all places." Capitol Hill, royal palace, great house. Even the richest of the rich, the "happiness is a gold bar" merchant princes with all their business acumen and corporate investments, were hit where it hurts.

There was no bread to be had. Anywhere, at any price.

No bread, no biscuits and honey, no crescent cakes for cosmic deities. No olive oil, no sheep's milk, no wine for libations to the Baals. No fatted calf, no milk-fed veal, no smoked fish from Galilee. No fancy gourmet foods. No sweet tooth pacifiers.

No health food nuts.

When famine struck . . .

Some of the people hoarded a handful of meal and a little oil in a cruse against the day they would die. Some scraped the bottom of the barrel and fell on hard times. Some stole, some starved. Some sold themselves to the "company store."

Some of the people experienced bitter new gastronomical taste sensations. Some gathered poison-fruited wild gourds: "There is death in the pot!" Some fought wild dogs for scraps; some contested with harvester ants for wild seeds. Some blasphemed God and died.

Some turned to astrologer-priests. Some turned to nature gods. Some, to human sacrifice. Others, to cannibalism.

In the Great Famine (in the reign of King Jehoram), when Ben-hadad, king of Syria, mustered his entire army outside Samaria and laid a siege, when economic ills gripped the land and lack of bread was a way of life, when inflation was the number one domestic problem and "an ass's head was sold for eighty shekels of silver and the fourth part of a kab of dove's dung for five shekels of silver"—mothers boiled and ate their children.

This was not of God!

At all times the door of hope was open. "If I send famine . . . if my people, which are called by my name, will humble themselves, and pray, and seek my face, and turn from their wicked ways; then will I hear from heaven, and will forgive their sin, and will heal their land."

Yet for all this, Israel did not return to the LORD.

WATER RIGHTS

"'And I also withheld the rain from you when there were yet three months to the harvest . . . yet you did not return to me,' says the LORD" (Amos 4:7a, 8c, RSV).

A tongue of drought licks moisture from the drying ground. Dust storms skim the prairie soil; dirt clods throw their weight around. Farm equipment lies buried under sand while tumbleweeds drift aimlessly about.

Range lands turn from green to brown. Cattle thirst; wildlife suffer. Water levels lower. Lakes dry out. "Gully washers" exist in memory alone.

A chance shower sprinkles one field and skips the next. It hits farmless foothills and misses crop-sown valleys. No matter. It is "too little too late." Seeds have already lost their growth.

In water-short parts of California, oat and barley dry farmers plough under burned-out crops. Where irrigation exists, lack of rain leaves alkaline salts in the unleached soil and crop yields are stunted.

Along the Rio Grande, through New Mexico and down into Texas drought finger-paints the land with gloom. In Southern Colorado, wheat farmers watch helplessly as rainless clouds float overhead. In Southern Utah, alfalfa withers and hopes for sorghum plantings fail.

SOW THE WIND

In stricken corn states, moisture supplies vanish as drought dehydrates sun-parched fields. Throughout the Great Plains, winter wheat crop failure hits as dry weather and disease take their toll.

Governors of stricken states ask millions in federal relief funds for disaster counties. Forest areas close as browning grasses become tinder dry. Even the national economy reels as cattlemen lose breeding stock and sell calves at half-weight, while consumers face beefed-up "market basket" reports.

In small communities, water tables become dangerously low and stringent rationing makes a gallon of water precious. In coastal areas, salt water intrusion threatens below-sea-level supplies, and a gallon of hauled-in water costs more than gasoline.

Malcontents blame the weatherman, and climatologists project future damage. Rainmakers (weather modifiers) seed the clouds with silver iodide crystals, and environmentalists question the ethics of weather-tinkering. "Is it nice to fool 'Mother Nature'?"

Ancient Israel employed some very down-to-earth water conservation measures. When the prospect of drought threatened the land, she was not without resources. Naturally, she did not enjoy the sophistication of present-day water systems. Unknown to her were the advances in modern Palestine: the water research programs, development of drip irrigation methods, conversion of salt water into fresh through flash and freeze processes and purification of brackish ground waters.

Unknown to her as well were the green-thumb conveniences of water gadgetry. She had no time clocks to turn sprinklers on and off. No metal root feeders to maintain the right underground moisture level for her ornamental trees; no soakers to ooze water on the soil. Even King Ahab, for all his lofty ways, was without a watering wand to douse the hanging baskets in his latticed garden.

But Israel, especially the Northern Kingdom, was in no way lacking: *she had an overhead sprinkler system bar none.* From seedtime through harvest, early and latter rains graced the land with life-giving showers; throughout the long, hot summer, a neighborly west wind imported "heavenly dews" that made living not only possible, but pleasant as well. Best of all, there was no charge for these services: God footed the bill Himself.

In addition, Israel had to her advantage a number of time-proved methods for retaining the rain water God sent her way. Deep-set wells, easily accessible to bucket and rope, brought spring rain water back to the earth's surface. Large storage pools located adjacent to kitchen gardens and dams strategically placed above contoured hillside terraces upgraded her water supplies immeasurably. Rock-hewn cisterns (narrow mouthed to prevent surface evaporation and generously cemented to discourage underground seepage) collected the fallout of winter floodwaters. In fact, Ms. Samaria was so amply supplied with limestone cisterns to catch and hold the raindrops falling on her pretty head, in time of siege she had a distinct advantage over her water-shy foes.

There was no end to Israel's liquid-lifeline blessings! Hillside springs naturally came to her aid. Rock-walled ravines trapped hidden streams for her use. Moreover, an ingenious system of man-made channels, furrows and troughs enabled any farmer with a little savvy to control the flow of water through his fields—by damming up or breaking down the tractable soil with his bare feet.

Yet in spite of all this, it wasn't always easy for Israel to be green. Drought was an ever-present possibility.

When heaven-sent rains refreshed the fields with well-timed drenching, when flash floods covered sandy riverbeds with tumbling waters, when early morning dews caressed the soil with drops of cooling moisture: then Israel blossomed like a rose.

But when clouds without rain passed high overhead and riverbeds ran dry, when moisture levels bit the dust and the earth cried out through parched, cracked lips: then Israel browned and all but wasted away.

Then tender young growing greens hung their heads in mourning, and bewildered cattle thirsted the landscape over. Then men wandered to-and-fro in rootless confusion, like tumbleweeds tossed by the wind.

It would seem that ordeal by drought would awaken Israel to her dependence upon God. *It would seem the discipline of the overhead shutoff valve* would bring her to her senses and force her to acknowledge the sovereign rights of God.

But no. God withheld rain times without number; yet Israel did not return to the Lord.

God withheld rain in the fall season, when cool damp air rising off the still-hot ground triggers thunderstorms, when "former rains" are needed to revive parched soil and soften it for wheat plantings: yet Israel did not return to the Lord.

God withheld rain in the winter months, when melons and summer grains are planted, when steady downpours fill pools and cisterns to overflowing and torrential storms flash flood rivers and streams: yet Israel did not return to the Lord.

God withheld rain in the spring of the year, when winter crops reach their peak and summer crops further their growth, when rapid temperature changes usher out the season with harvest-guaranteeing storms: yet Israel did not return to the Lord.

God withheld dew in summer, when vegetable and fruit gardens come to the fore, when summer grains ripen and olives and grapes look to harvest: yet Israel did not return to the Lord.

As the God of Judgment, God sent rain upon one city and no rain upon another city; one field would be rained upon, and the field on which it did not rain withered. Two or three cities wandered to one city to drink water and were not satisfied: yet Israel did not return to the Lord.

As the God of Grace, God gave Israel the right to apply pressure to the overhead shutoff valve at any time: "If I shut up heaven that there be no rain. . . .

"If my people, which are called by my name, shall humble themselves, and pray, and seek my face, and turn from their wicked ways, then will I hear from heaven, and will forgive their sin, and will heal their land."

Yet for all this, Israel did not return to the Lord.

FIELDS OF CONTENTION

"'I smote you with blight and mildew; I laid waste your gardens and your vineyards; your fig trees and your olive trees the locust devoured; yet you did not return to me,' says the LORD" (Amos 4:9, RSV).

A roving band of gypsy moths gnaws on green leaves in concert, filling the night air with unwelcome, rain-like sounds. By morning, acres of trees will be defoliated, and irreparable damage will have been done. Still, the band plays on.

In central California, marching columns of half-inch-long

carpenter ants topple giant Sequoia trees (among the oldest and largest living things on earth). To the south, elm leaf beetles, elm bark beetles, spring caterpillars, sap-sucking aphids, twig-snapping ants, sooty mold fungus and honey-dew-dripping European elm scale gang up on drought-stricken elms. In a nearby college town, dusky-footed wood rats threaten to reduce a famed botanic garden to scrub.

Throughout the land, after-the-fall environmental strug-gles intensify with the advent of unseasonable weather. Spring cold snaps, premature fall frosts, fruit-stripping winds and hail increase the strife.

Nor does the approach of warm weather help. With rising heat and humidity levels, the battlefield enlarges: mildew spores germinate, nematodes activate; viruses cause leaf roll and plants "catch" diseases.

In Florida, "lethal yellowing" wastes palm fronds almost overnight; in Northern California, brown rot (fungus) sneaks up on early cling peaches; in rose gardens along the coast, rose leaf rust and powdery mildew turn harried gardeners gray.

All-out pesticide attacks open further problem-fields of contention. Indiscriminate crop-dusting, the "shotgun approach" to insecticide spraying (whereby beneficial insects and harmless wildlife suffer) and "kill and over-kill" bug-bombings all have foes in increasing numbers. With the passage of time, field workers claim adverse health effects from pesticides; crops wither from chemical over-dose, and bugs develop resistance to even the deadliest poisons.

As civilization spreads, the field wars heighten. Genetic erosion threatens certain food crops. Urban smog wafts its strange chemistry over rural areas, and unknown air pollu-tants wipe out leafy growth.

The "slashing axes of advancing society" fell ancient oaks without conscience, and "progress" bulldozes century-old groves of eucalyptus trees in a single day.

The dirt farmer of ancient Israel had much with which to contend. If it wasn't ordeal by drought that disturbed the land, then it was excessive rainfall. A cyclonic storm that overshot the Levant Coast, a blustery downpour that caused untold dam-age from flash flood runoff and erosion.

Or if not rain, then an unseasonable cold weather front brought problems. A rare frost in the higher, grape-laden hills; a hail-storm that attacked the flax crop on the eve of harvest—heaven-sent missiles targeting on the fluffy white bolls.

If it wasn't so dry even puddle-jumping frogs gave up and croaked, then unwelcome birds and beasts visited the fields *en masse*. Migrating turtledoves helped themselves to seeds and clover. Destructive peacocks strutted their stuff through kitchen gardens. Nomadic herds of goats feasted at will on the pristine landscape; golden-colored "little foxes" spoiled the vines of sweet-juiced grapes, and mice marauders marred the land by root crop gnawing.

And if this were not enough—snails, slugs and related crea-tures of the night ate anything green and succulent; while har-vester ants added to their seed collection daily—litter-bugging a telltale trail of throwaway husks wherever they went.

At times, the malaise of the land knew no bounds. Scorching east winds from oven-hot deserts blasted all vegetation—laying waste gardens and vineyards alike. Then again blight struck, or mildew fungi stunted seed growth—leaving the five o'clock stubble on the face of the earth as sickly as the grasses that thatched the rooftops of the poor.

But none of these things attacked the outcroppings of the land as did the locusts. In a locust invasion, nothing escaped. Leaves, bark, roots, husks, stubble. *They ate the whole thing!* For when "after the manner of Egypt" locust visitations judged the land; when spring fever drove billions of hungry young locusts toward Palestine, and "flying squadrons" of whirring-winged creatures suddenly darkened the atmosphere, eclipsing the noonday sun and filling the air with crop-dusting excrement; when invading troops of mass-coordinated locusts parachuted to the defenseless land, entering and searching every dwelling while citizens fell back in horror; when devouring locust armies inched over every green thing: biting, chewing and consuming with strip-mining voraciousness; when trees stood naked and plant life disappeared for miles around; when heaps of rotting locust bodies befouled the air and famine and pestilence made the scene—then the fields of the Valley of Jezreel foreshadowed Armageddon.

It would seem these life-and-death battles for the outcrop-pings of the fields should have awakened Israel to the greatness of God and the frailty of man. "All flesh is grass, and all its beauty is like the flower of the field. The grass withers, the flower fades, when the breath of the LORD blows upon it. . . ."

It would seem the most self-sufficient man-of-the-fields should have realized his need of something more than a compost heap to fall back on when environmental catastrophe laid him low. Even the prophet Jonah listened (albeit angrily) when God spoke to him through a sultry east wind, a scorching Middle East sun and an eager-beaver wireworm that nibbled the underpinnings of his pet gourd. But no! When the fig tree failed to blossom and the labor of the olive failed, Israel did not return to God.

Instead, she turned to her ecological deities.

In this, she was like the former tenant of the land, the oak-strong Amorite whom God cut down for the preservation of the human race. "I destroyed his fruit above and his roots beneath."

In this, she was becoming as degenerate as her Canaanite predecessors, thus endangering her future as a "nation under God." For the true contenders for the fields were not the birds and beasts, the "crawlies" and flying insects—*these were only the visible, material manifestation of an invisible, spiritual conflict.* The true contenders were the powers behind the thrones: the satanic forces behind the substitute-rival gods Israel enthroned in her heart.

Thus, it was *Satan vs. Jehovah* when Israel reared altars in the freshly seeded fields—altars of shame to Baal, "the Lord of the Skies," and to Asherah, "the Queen of Heaven."

It was *Satan vs. Jehovah* when Israel prostrated herself before her erotic fertility gods—writhing on the ground in licentious rites, through "sacred sex acts" seeking to encourage her lusting deities to sexual intercourse in high places, that by "sympathetic magic" the land might bring forth fruit for Baal.

It was *Satan vs. Jehovah* when Israel flagellated herself in ritualistic ecstasy—bloodying the fields, mouthing demonic utterances, wailing "O Baal, hear us. . . ."

And it was Jehovah vs. Satan when God answered—by fire, by storm, by drought, by pestilence and by locust invasion.

At any time, Israel could have heeded *God's Environmental Impact Report*: "If there be dearth in the land, if there be pestilence, if there be blasting, or mildew, locusts, or caterpillars. . . .

"If my people, who are called by my name, shall humble themselves, and pray, and seek my face, and turn from their wicked ways; then will I hear from heaven, and will forgive their sin, and will heal their land."

   Yet for all this, Israel did not return to the Lord.

THE PARTING OF THE WAYS

". . . how can we walk together with your sins between us?"
(Amos 3:3, TLB).

ACTS OF GOD
THE THEATRE OF WAR
FIREBRANDS
THE "NO-RETURNS"
THE PARTING OF THE WAYS

ACTS OF GOD

"'I overthrew some of you, as when God overthrew Sodom and Gomorrah . . . yet you did not return to me,' says the LORD" (Amos 4:11a, RSV).

At precisely 6:01 a.m., a man awakens from a sound sleep. He feels at once alert, yet dazed.

The earth is shaking. The floor is moving. The ceiling of his room is webbed with cracks. His bed has cast him out; his bookshelf has turned on him; his fallen book-club specials are roughing him up. He is helpless. Defenseless. As vulnerable as a city broken into and left without walls.

He cannot handle his situation or himself. He is no more able to control his heaving emotions than the thin-lipped coping that edges his swimming pool is able to contain its sloshing waters. He is overwhelmed. He feels as shattered as his sliding glass door, as shaken as his family room chandelier, as broken up as his red-tiled patio floor.

To top it all off, above the disquieting barking of his

frightened dogs, he hears the cry of his little boy. "Daddy, do something!"

California is not the only state to have its faults. Places once thought immune to quakes now shudder from the earth's crustal motion. Quake activity is slight. But still . . .
Already in the twentieth century, the earth's disturbing predilection for shifting has left a trail of trauma. Earthquakes in such "divers places" as Alaska, San Francisco and the Hawaiian Islands have rudely jolted the needle on the Richter scale. In the Yellowstone National Park, a nearly fifteen mile long fault scarp mutely testifies to a night of horror—when age-old stresses twenty miles beneath the earth's surface suddenly snapped, a towering mountain collapsed, a lake tilted, active geysers failed midstream, and once-quiet hot pools erupted violently.

And now for the "Big One"!

God called to His runaway nation, Israel, but she did not listen. God spoke to her heart in a still small voice, but she did not answer.

God positioned His "advisory signboard" prophets directly in her collision-course path to flag her down, but she did not heed their warnings. God sent *after-the-manner-of-Egypt* pestilence and plague, the slow panic of drought and famine, crop failure and economic depression to rumble strip her way, but she did not turn back to Him. Rather, she turned to her "nothing" gods.
Undaunted, God sent limited after-the-manner-of-Sodom-and-Gomorrah instant-jeopardy judgments to jolt her to her senses before she reached the point of no return.

Wind, earthquake, fire. The drama of the Northern Kingdom unfolded before a backdrop of these and other "acts of God." In the ninth century B.C., especially in the days of the prophets Elijah and Elisha, the saga of the nation was played out on "disaster sets" that would delight the heart and challenge the special effect skills of any Hollywood producer.
There were winds. Cyclonic storms, east winds, whirlwinds. Winds where the sound level rivaled that of the hurricane-force, earsplitting, rock-throwing melee at the Yellowstone site; where the damage done approached that of a Midwest twister, a

Texas killer tornado or a Louisiana coast-lashing hurricane.

There were earthquakes. Blockbusting earthquakes *a la San Francisco*—with the traditional after-the-earthquake sequences of panic and fire. There were holocausts—fiery holocausts with tinder-dry plains devastated by uncontained, scorched-earth policy flames that devoured the land, leaving nothing for locust invaders.

Surely, it would not be right to assume that all convulsive "act of God" disasters occurring in Israel were designed as warning judgments on the land. Some were, some were not. Many came from so-called "natural causes"; the impersonal cause-and-effect operation of divinely ordained laws of nature.

But whatever the elemental cause behind an "act of God," whatever the geographical area singled out, the extent of damage, the body count—the disaster called the nation to repentance lest the whole land likewise perish.

It was a massive stroke given in grace to bring the nation to its knees—that a final-stroke judgment might be averted.

In a sense it was strange Israel did not take her jarring Sodom-and-Gomorrah disasters more seriously, for she had set up housekeeping deep in the heart of earthquake country.

Beneath her feet lay a *terra rossa* foundation of crisscrossing structural lines—a rough flooring of massive upfolds and downfolds, oblique hinge-faults, upwarped domes and depressed basins. On her northern terrace, a gigantic fault scarp defined the boundaries of forested Upper Galilee and vine-ladened Lower Galilee. To the south, the Jerusalem-based Mount of Olives (which will one day quake at the triumphant return of the victorious Christ with His saints) straddled a treelined geological fault.

Moreover, by her side stretched the parallel-faulted Great Rift—that swelling and cracking, faulting and settling gash that spans a fifth of the earth's circumference (from Lebanon to the heart of Africa) and raises mile-high ridges in Palestine (thus flooring the Jordan Valley and sinking the Dead Sea).

And as if these things hadn't shaken them enough, down the road from Israel was the place where Abraham stood centuries before and looked toward the cities of the Dead Sea plain —only to see the smoke of that country going up "as the smoke of a furnace."

For on that historic day, Sodom and Gomorrah, Admah and Zeboim mushroomed into eternity. On that day, their cup of iniquity brimmed full and a final "act of God" catapulted their society into instant nothingness. Using the elements at hand—which scholars and geologists indicate were a subterranean lake of oil and gas beneath Sodom, petroleum seepages, slime (asphalt) pits, a thick stratum of salt, free sulphur, volcanic agencies, the movable rift fault line and the crater-like Dead Sea depression—*God came up with a sky-high doomsday eruption* that literally rained "brimstone and fire from the Lord out of heaven."

As in a moment, God overthrew their cities, destroyed their civilization and salted their once-fertile land. When He was through, there was nothing left. No life. No remnant. No rubble. Nothing. Not even an "X" to mark the spot.

Possibly too many years of mild "Daddy, *do something*" tremors had lulled Israel into a false sense of security.

In any event, for all this she did not return to the Lord.

THE THEATRE OF WAR

"'While your horses were captured I cut down your young men with the sword; And I made the stench of your camps fill your nostrils. And yet,' says the Lord, 'you have not returned to me'" (Amos 4:10b, Phillips).

Year after year, the theatre of war stages hot wars and cold wars, all-out wars and limited wars, undeclared wars, pull-out wars and no-win wars. . . .

In the spring, that was when kings went to war in ancient Palestine. It was not that a *rite of spring* spectacular was needed to officially open the theatre of war, but that the spring season finally made troop movement on the rough terrain possible.

For in an uphill, down-dale land of rutted dirt roads without bridges, a land of narrow gauge mountain trails and waterlogged marshland depressions, of forests so impenetrable they "devoured more people than the sword" and of thorn-covered Mediterranean maquis (scrub) so entangling troops became confused and lost all sense of direction—in such a land, the battle scenes were of necessity carefully staged and timed, or everyone lost.

Only along the coastal plains of the Levant, the valleys of Jordan and Jezreel (Esdraelon, Armageddon) and the steppe lands of Bashan was movement of men and equipment un-hindered by the lay of the land. Obviously, such heavy military equipment as horse-drawn battle chariots, catapults for hurling arrows and stones over the ramparts of a besieged city and wall-breaching battering rams of such heft up to two hundred men were needed to lift the beam—all these required wide-open spaces to maneuver. Thus, only in a few places was large-scale mechanized warfare possible let alone profitable.

As it was, though King Solomon made a name for himself with a razzle-dazzle horse-and-chariot force (importing pedigreed war steeds from Asia Minor and fielding no less than fourteen hundred chariots and twelve thousand skilled horsemen)—the majority of Israel's kings were content with a lower budg-eted, more modest display of pass-by strength.

So on the whole it was the lowly foot soldier who saved the military day for Israel; whether by occupying a strategic hill-top, fighting for a Jordan ford or defending a vital corridor of land. It was the mud-slogging infantryman with his bronzed battle-ax, the unerring archer with his highflying arrows, the muscled downward-thrusting spearman, the Saul-like javelin thrower and the Davidic "slinger of stones" with his right-or-left-hand dexterity who raised the curtain on the Middle East war theatre with battle scenes ranging from full-scale campaigns employing "a cast of thousands" to one-to-one, fight-to-the-finish contests.

Now on the rare occasion when Ephraim-Israel went forth to battle armed with valor; and with courage and commitment to the national cause fought for her land, her loved ones and her God—she enjoyed peace at all sides. She walked with head held high and conducted her international affairs from a position of honor.

But when the lady sophisticate denied her God and lowered her eyes from the Lord of hosts, she suffered defeat on the battlefield. Her vision of right and wrong clouded, and "peace not war" unrealities captured her thoughts.

Instead of clean-cut victories, she became enmeshed in a series of ill-fated military misadventures.

Her troops were committed to no-win brush wars. Her bor-ders changed places more often than a floating crap game. Ig-nominious and disorderly retreats were the order of the day. Her horses were captured; the flower of her youth was slain, and the stench of death filled her camps.

Her honor was violated by "hired lover" allies; her freedoms were denied, and her land was ground beneath the military heel of her conquerors.

Yet for all this, Israel did not return to the Lord.

FIREBRANDS

"'. . . you were as a brand plucked out of the burning; yet you did not return to me,' says the Lord" (Amos 4:11b, RSV).

An elderly resident of a foothill-located rest home wanders off on his own. Confused and disoriented, he soon becomes lost in a nearby mountain area.

Days later, a hiker finds him huddled under a clump of bushes. He is weak but still alive. Help is summoned; members of a Search and Rescue Team come to his aid. But even as his blanket-wrapped body is placed on a litter, fire breaks out. In a moment, flames rage all around!

Undaunted, the rescuers lift the litter high, dodge the flames and scramble down the mountain—carrying the man to a place of safety. The litter is scorched, the blanket smells of smoke, but the man is still alive.

It would appear he has "lucked out" once more.

By rights, wrong-way Israel should have been huddled under a clump of bushes by the time Amos arrived on the Northern Kingdom scene. After a century and a half of prophetic sig-alerts, hard-way chastenings and earthshaking judgments, she should have been in a state of near collapse. After exposure to elements of famine, pestilence and sword, out-of-sight economic inflation, bottom-of-the-barrel depression, drought, flood, wind and fire, she should have had her eyebrows singed at least.

But no. The decade Amos came to the Northern Kingdom, Israel was alive and well—and living in a golden age of peace and prosperity. She was riding high, at the peak of her popularity. Neighbor nations looked up to her. Foreign traders cast pots of gold at her feet. Her own nobility luxuriated in ivory-tower ease.

Israel had not only survived the divine judgments of God, she had come through smelling like a rose!

In grace, God had delivered her from the consequences of her own folly. In grace, He had snatched her, as a brand from the burning, out of every disaster that threatened to consume her. In grace, He had lifted her to new heights!

Contrary to all appearance, Israel had not "lucked out" as a nation—she had been *plucked out* of her fiery extremities by God.

The narrow escapes, near misses and skin-of-the-teeth deliverances she enjoyed would have put to shame many an old-time Saturday matinee cliff-hanger. Each succeeding episode of "The Perils of Israel" would have made even angels sit on the edge of their seats (figuratively speaking) and gasp "What next?"

What next indeed! Time and again, just when Israel lay flat on her back in utter helplessness, and hope was all but gone— *God entered the picture* and brought her through to safety.

When the shutoff valve of the overhead sprinkler jammed and there was not a cloud in sight, when moisture levels bit the dust and frenzied cries to Baal only precipitated a crisis—*God intervened* with a downpour that drenched the nation's breadbasket, filled the cisterns and revived all living things.

When the Great Famine devoured the population of besieged Samaria and bread was not to be found, when the nation dangled precariously on the brink of extinction and vultures circled overhead in holding patterns—*God made* the besieging Syrian army "hear the sound of chariots and of horses, the sound of a great army . . ." thus alarming them so much they panicked and fled—leaving a trail of food, garments and equipment behind.

Upon seeing this, the astonished Israelites braved outside their gates, plundered the abandoned enemy camp and followed the trail of throwaway goods to the banks of the Jordan (no doubt laughing all the way).

The "pluck outs" of God were no less delightful and ingenious when Israel played her battle scenes. Natural cause "acts of God" were frequently sent for her deliverance (as well as discipline). A sudden shift in wind, a fortuitous D-day fog cover, a flash flood that bogged down enemy equipment—these were among the elemental "turn of affairs" brought about by the Lord.

Again, when the kings of Judah and Edom joined Israel in an attempt to regain lost territory from Moab, a circuitous march of seven days left their armies faint with thirst. That night there was no wind or rain, but in the morning water coming from the direction of Edom filled the dry stream beds around their bivouac. When the Moabites rose that morning, and the sun shone upon the water, the water appeared to them "as red as blood." Assuming the allied armies had fought among themselves and slaughtered one another, the unsuspecting Moabites rushed the Israelite camp for spoil—only to find themselves surrounded, outnumbered, outwitted and out of luck!

But all these "firebrand" deliverances given Israel were as nothing to the decades-long *Search and Rescue* operation God staged from the days of King Jehoahaz on. Just when it seemed the nation had breathed her last, when a mere handful of footmen, horsemen and chariots stood between her and THE END— the Lord turned toward Israel. The Lord's "arrow of victory" was given to the turn-of-the-century monarch, Jehoash, and his son, the mighty warrior-king, Jeroboam II, was raised up as the nation's rescuer. By his hand the Lord saved them, that the name of Israel would not be blotted out from under heaven.

Yet for all this, Israel did not return to the Lord.

THE "NO-RETURNS"

"'. . . yet you did not return to me,' says the Lord" (Amos 4:11c, RSV).

A major disaster rocks the nation, shocking it to its senses, lowering it to its knees. Hearts are saddened, thoughts disquieted.

At the height of the crisis, a potential victim despairs for his life. He lies trapped under a protective covering that threatens to give way at any moment. He can breathe and think, but that is all.

His mind wanders back to long-forgotten childhood scenes: a class in Sunday School, the story of Sodom and Gomorrah, the Bible verse, "Be not deceived; God is not mocked: for whatsoever a man soweth, that shall he also reap." He recalls his teacher's words, "God will not allow anyone to rebel against Him indefinitely. The cities of the plain had rejected Him for the last time. Now they would reap what they had sown."

He wonders what is ahead for him. Will he end up as a statistic? Or will he be plucked out "as a brand from the burning"? He vows that if he lives he will return to the Lord and get right with Him.

At long last, a rescue team unearths him—weak, but still

alive. Alive enough to give a brief, on-the-scene inter-view to a local reporter; alive enough to appear on a T.V. talk show twenty-four hours later; alive enough to go to church the following Sunday and hear: "The hand of God could not possibly be behind the recent disaster. God has no part in such calamitous events. We are to quiet our fears and restructure our thoughts."

Upon hearing this, the man heaves a sigh of relief, con-gratulates himself on His providential "stroke of luck," dismisses God from his thoughts and wanders off on his own once more.

Several times, Israel took tentative steps in the direction of the Lord. On occasion, her kings lowered themselves to take battle-scene marching orders. On Mount Carmel, she even acknowledged, "The LORD, He is God! The LORD, He is God!"

But on the whole, when her flat-on-the-back crises were over and her energy had been restored once more, Israel went back to her old ways, her old speed and her old dream world unreali-ties.

Her turnings were brief and of the easy on/off flippancy of a toggle switch.

For all this, she did not return to the Lord.

THE PARTING OF THE WAYS

"Can two walk together, except they be agreed?" (Amos 3:3).

A couple agrees to go their separate ways.

It must have been awkward for Israel to be a "nation under God." It must have been downright uncomfortable at times.

Just when she was about to kick up her heels, *there God was*, underfoot. Just when she was ready to throw over all restraints and take off on her own, *there God was*, in the way. Just when she was about to partake of the more delicious aspects of for-bidden fruit, *there God was*, looking over her shoulder.

There He was—all the time! He entered into her affairs, un-asked. He spoke up, even when He was not spoken to. He warned her of the payoff of sin, even when she would rather not know.

Worst of all, He was always right.

90

What to do with such a God? He was impossible to have around!

When she altered her life pattern to fit her dream world, *there He was*, cramping her style. When she spaced out via the vine, *there He was*, with His little white line.

When she entertained lavishly after the manner of Ahab, wining and dining the enemies of God with open-armed hospitality, when in the name of brotherhood she joined avowed God-haters in "I am as you are" toasts, *there He was*, a resident party pooper!

Of course there were times when it was nice to have a God around the house. Times when there were problems to work through, burdens to bear, messes to clean up and trash to be carried out. Crisis times when the riverbed plumbing overflowed, the kitchen garden flooded and the economy washed out.

To be sure, He was handy to have on call in times of emergency, disaster or loss. And when she suffered flat-on-the-back helplessness, He was always compassionate and kind. At all times He was faithful, gracious, generous and loving.

But aside from that . . .

Who asked Him to be Lord and Master over her?
What right did he have to direct her life, dictate the conditions of her abiding in the land and define the terms "right and wrong," "good and evil," for her life?

Just who did He think He was anyway?

He was the Holy One . . . who had had it with Israel!
"Listen, I groan under the burden of you, as a wagon creaks under a full load."

God had had enough. It was impossible for the present arrangement to continue any longer. He could care for Israel and love her with an everlasting love; He could watch over Israel and rescue her from the consequences of her own folly.

Indeed, if Israel so desired, He could even deliver her from bondage to "The Jeroboam Follies!"

But nothing could be done with the folly of "no-return."

If Israel refused to return to the Lord her God, there was no way the rift between them could be healed. If she would not heed the "Lion's Roar" message of Amos, she would reach the parting of the ways.

If she then continued to walk contrary to Him, she would walk right out of the land. *He would be in residence, she would not.* There would be no common ground, no line of communication, no place of meeting between them.

Their life patterns would be incompatible, their differences irreconcilable. Their relationship terminated.

Their only agreement would be to go their separate ways.

THE SECURITY OF FOOLS

"Do not the people of the city tremble when the alarm is sounded?" (Amos 3:6a, Phillips).

WHAT IS HAPPENING?
AN ADVERSARY
THE LESSONS OF HISTORY
THE DOUBLE STANDARD
THE SECURITY OF FOOLS

WHAT IS HAPPENING?

"Can a city suffer disaster unless the Lord is its cause?" (Amos 3:6b, Phillips).

A man lifts the sports section from the morning paper and tosses the remainder aside. What is happening in and to his country?
At times he would rather not know.

God is a God of order, not disorder; of cause-and-effect, not happenstance. He is a God of basic "whatever a man sows, that he will also reap" laws concerning mankind; of "what goes up, must come down" laws concerning proud, ungodly nations.

The Northern Kingdom of Israel was just such a nation. Yet surprisingly enough, the men of Israel were fully aware of the existence of divine sow-and-reap laws. Indeed their existence depended upon the unalterable certainty of just such laws. They knew that when they planted wheat, they harvested wheat;

when they planted barley, they harvested barley—not millet or corn.

These things they understood. But when their inner cities cropped an upsurge of disaster, when their streets sprouted offshoots of terror, they were at a loss as to the root cause.

What was happening in *and to* their land?

To help the nation interpret these "signs of the times" properly, Amos made a straight-from-the-shoulder, common sense pitch to the proud nobles assembled at the Bethel shrine.

"Can two walk together unless they have agreed to do so?" he asked. Obviously, the answer was "no." *Unless the two were of a single mind, their steps would lead in opposite directions.*

In rapid succession, Amos directed two additional questions. "Does a lion roar in the forest when there is no prey for him? Or the young lion growl in his lair if he has made no kill?"

To up-the-ladder men, long familiar with the basic bite-and-devour laws of the jungle, the situation Amos sketched was equally clear. *No. The majestic king of beasts did not thunder his authority without cause, nor did the young lion growl with mouth-watering anticipation unless a paw-licking repast was in the offing.*

Again Amos threw out two related questions. "Does a bird fall to the ground unless it is caught? Does the trap fly up when there is no bird to catch?"

Once more the men of Israel were on familiar ground. The simple teaching-picture of bird and trap was not new to them. They had often set cleverly hinged traps for twig-hopping sparrows, or scattered grain along noose-concealed bird runs or spread entangling nets over wind-grounded quail.

Poor birds! Never again would they fly free. The fowler would deliver them to the marketplace; the merchant would tag them for quick sale, and the family man would cart them home as caged pets for his children.

Suddenly Amos threw the men of Israel a curve. Without warning he went from the known to the unknown, from the physical realm to the spiritual. With the inherent skill of a natural born teacher, he led the august assembly before him to a close-to-home, street-level scene. "Do not the people of the city tremble when the alarm is sounded?

"Can a city suffer disaster unless the Lord is its cause?"

At last Amos touched the men of Israel where they lived. *Now their lives* were in danger, not the lives of helpless prey. *Their liberties* were at stake, not those of hapless sparrows.

The disorders flourishing in their cities, the ungodliness, the outcroppings of violence and crime, these were not mere happenstance but the direct consequence of turning from God.

The under-the-vine drunkenness, the lawsuits springing up like weeds in the furrows of the field, the overnight mushrooming of alternate lifestyles, these were but *visible fruit of invisible plantings* of root rebellion against the Lord.

In parting company with the sovereignty of God, the men of Israel had unwittingly removed themselves from divine blessing and placed themselves under alternate laws of cursing. What was now "happening" was only the first fruits of what might yet come.

If they sowed the wind, might they not be grounded by the whirlwind? If they consumed everything in their path, might they not be caught in the fowler's snare? If they twig-hopped between God and Baal, might they not trigger a calamity?

Might they not be delivered to the marketplace, slave-tagged for quick sale and carried off to a foreign land as prisoners?

Poor Ephraim-Israel! Then never again would they soar the heights of freedom; never again would they come and go at will.

Sadly enough, it would seem the men of Israel never made a direct connection between apostasy from God and subsequent national disaster.

Either they would rather not know what was happening in *and to* their country, or they didn't care; or they were so wrapped up in their own sectioned interest, they saw and heard nothing—not even the voice of God as it was printed daily on the pages of their times.

AN ADVERSARY

"Therefore thus says the Lord GOD: 'An adversary shall surround the land, and bring down your defenses from you, and your strongholds shall be plundered"' (Amos 3:11, RSV).

A man wonders what is ahead for his country . . .

Amos was a positive man. There was nothing vague or wishy-washy about him. His questions were no-nonsense links between men and reality; his statements were authoritative outbursts prefaced by "Now hear this" commands; his prophecies were so sure of fulfillment they could only reach their certain end with "This is it" periods.

Therefore, his prophecy concerning Israel's future, if the "Lion's Roar" message fell on deaf ears, was a positive one.

A positive negative!

If the Northern Kingdom continued to walk away from God, the relationship between the two would strain beyond the breaking point. The Holy One of Israel would no longer be in the midst as Guardian and Protector, Lover and Provider, but as Adversary and Judge. No longer would He comfort her in times of sorrow, or deliver her from painful consequences or snatch her "as a brand from the burning" out of fiery extremities. The "pluck out" days would be over; the "Perils of Israel" would have reached THE END. There would be no sequels. No revivals. It would be FINIS.

And that was not all. If Israel persisted in her wrong-way collision course, if she refused to allow rumble-strip experiences to jolt her to reality; she would be swept up in a stream of oncoming events over which she would have little or no control. Eventually, she would pass the point of no return; the countdown would begin; the days of her existence would be numbered.

Time would be her enemy, not her friend. The budding first fruits of root rebellion against the Lord would mature to full-blown harvests. The law of causality would be in effect; the laws of national disintegration would operate. There would be no going back, only forward to a certain end.

If the "Lion's Roar" warning Amos thundered went unheeded, Israel could only reach her certain end with death by military defeat. No longer would the Northern Kingdom be a "nation under God." No longer would it be a nation. No longer would it exist.

In newsreel black and white, Amos foretold the future to the men assembled at the idol altar at Bethel. As though presenting a documentary before the act, he unfolded the who, what, when, where and why of the nation's impending fall.

If Israel would not repent, she would come to a bitter end. God Himself would be her adversary. Her foremost enemy, her primary foe. "Behold, I, the Lord GOD, have my eyes on this sinful kingdom, and I will wipe it off the face of the earth. I will destroy . . . I will slay . . . I will deliver up the city. . . ."

If God were against Israel, who could be for her?

No one would be for her. Least of all her "hired lovers." They would have long since moved on to greener pastures, there to court the good graces of neighbor nations more up-and-coming than she. Nations rising to prominence—even as she fell.

Thus shunned and forsaken by her fair-weather friends, she would add to loneliness *fear*. Not only would the Divine Adversary be against her, there would be a secondary adversary as well. An enemy nation raised up by God as the instrument of His wrath: a whip nation, the rod of His anger. "Oh Israel, I will bring against you a nation that will bitterly oppress you from your northern boundary to your southern tip. . . ."

That nation would be much like Israel. Proud and ungodly; insatiable in its lusts. Materialism would be its God, love for Number One its Master. It would be cruel, animalistic in nature. Like a lion sunning itself in the tall grasses of the Jordan pride, it would set its eye upon the sinful kingdom for evil and not for good. It would bide its time and watch and wait. Like a young lion growling in its lair it would eye the well-fed land with mouth-watering anticipation. It would sieze the moment and pounce and kill.

Like Israel, that nation would act in accordance with its own will. It would face alternatives, make decisions and follow its chosen path free from divine coercion. Without knowing (much less caring) that it was doing the sovereign will of God, it would wipe the Northern Kingdom off the face of the earth.

At no time would God violate the free will or force the path of either nation. As the Divine Adversary, He would merely remove restraint from the lion and withdraw protection from the prey. In due time, His will would be done.

Slowly, steadily, surely, Israel would come to THE END.

Now hear this, Oh men of Israel! Give heed, you inhabitants of the land! You need not wonder what is ahead for your country. This is how it will be:

"An enemy is coming!"
From the northern boundary to the southern tip, all the way from Hamath to the brook of Arabah, the battle cry goes forth.
"Sound the alarm! They are coming!"

We are overwhelmed. The enemy descends upon us like a flood. The whole land trembles and shakes. It rises like the River Nile at flood time; it surges, seethes and subsides like the River of Egypt. We are left desolate in the wake.

Hamath is fallen. Hamath is ours no more. Once the mighty Jeroboam annexed Hamath to our borders, but now it it gone into captivity. Not Hamath only; Hazor stands empty. The people have fled in haste. Looms are threaded, tools are at hand, vessels await the next meal—but no one is there. The palace is gutted, the citadel devastated. Charred embers choke the air; thick ash enshrouds the land. There is no life, no hope left in Hazor.

What is happening? We are taken by surprise. We looked for light, not darkness. We prepared for peace, not war. Like a lion, the enemy attacks our strongholds. Like a moth, he wears away our borders. We are falling apart as a nation, disintegrating, vanishing from off the face of the earth.

We are left without protection. Our swift warriors stumble in flight; our strong men weaken without warning. Even our fighting men cannot escape alive. Our archers are unable to stand their ground, the stout of heart among us tremble, and the best of our horsemen cannot outdistance the foe.

We have no heroes. No men of valor. At the trembling of a leaf, our armies drop their weapons and flee for their lives.

We are disheartened. Always before God has delivered us from our foes, but not now. It is as if we fled from a lion and a bear grabbed hold of us; as if we then escaped, ran home and leaned a hand on the wall—only to be bitten by a snake.

We mourn a lot. Wailing is in every courtyard; cries of woe fill our streets. Farm workers come to join the mourning; professional mourners lead in sorrowful laments. We don sackcloth and shave our heads; we grieve as for an only son.

The songs of the temple are turned to howlings. The vineyards drip tears, not wine. We build houses of hewn stone, but do not dwell in them. We send young men to war; but few of them return. The city that went forth a thousand has a hundred left, and that which went forth a hundred has ten left to the house of Israel. And if there are ten men left in one house, they die.

We are wasting away. The dead bodies are many. In every place they are cast forth in silence.

Our gods have cast us off. We cry, "O Baal, hear us!" But no
one answers. We swear by the goddess Asherah, but we are not
helped. The high places of Beth-aven have been destroyed;
the images are spoiled, the horns of the altar cut off. Nettles
possess our sanctuaries, thorns and thistles our tabernacles.

Gilgal has gone into exile. Bethel has come to naught. Those
who say, "As your god lives, O Dan!" or, "As the way of Beersheba lives . . ." are fallen, never to rise again.

We are all but gone. We are no more than two bits of bone, or
a torn piece of ear from the mouth of a lion . . .

*At the time Amos prophesied, the present tense of Israel's
fall was still in the future. The land had not yet expelled the
house of Israel, nor would it if they would but return to God.*

THE LESSONS OF HISTORY

"Cross over to Calneh and look at it . . . is your land any greater
than theirs?" (Amos 6:2, Phillips).

A young teen shoves his history book aside.
Why bother with all that? Who cares about the past?

Northern Israel need not go far afield to study the rise and fall
of great empires—she need only look around.

By and large, her location among the Fertile Crescent nations
could not have been more fortuitous for history lesson-learning.
It was no topographical error that placed her smack-dab in the
middle of Palestine, that centered her on the crossroads of the
ancient world and positioned her squarely on the land bridge
between the rivers Nile and Euphrates.

No one had better opportunity than she to observe the "what
goes up must come down" fate of proud ungodly nations—
whether tiny Levantine city-states or great imperial powers. No
one had greater reason than she to learn the lessons of history
and learn them well.

If Israel would "cross over to Calneh" (via the northern route
of the Great Trunk Road, the oasis of Damascus and the military
beaten path to Mesopotamian points beyond), she would see
the crumbling ruins of early Assyrian glory. Once the city of
Calneh (presumedly ancient Calah) was magnificent to behold—
colossal man-headed winged lions of stone guarded the daz-

zling alabaster-paneled palace of Ashurnaspiral II; resplendent images of the gods rode high in triumphal parades, borne aloft to sounds of tumult and shoutings. Once the Black Obelisk of Shalmaneser III commanded the place of honor in the great square—the famed black limestone pillar depicting in bold cuneiform inscriptions the dizzying heights to which ninth century B.C. Assyria ascended, and the humiliating depths to which Israel descended under Jehu, her tribute-bearing king.

Once Calneh was riding high on the Middle East teeter-totter, but not now. Now her gods had cast her off; her palaces lay in heaps, and the sands of time drifted aimlessly in her streets.

If Israel would go from Calneh to "great Hamath" (retrace her steps to Hazor, take a hard right, go through Dan, Abel, the valley of Inyon and on to the northernmost limits of Jeroboam II's holdings), she would discover the plight of a people caught smack-dab in the middle of a hotly-contested seesaw for power. She would see the ups and downs, the back and forth movements of an independent kingdom unseated when opposing empires jousted for control over its strategic geographic position. She would see a nation displaced and dislocated beyond all healing—because it had the misfortune to be in the way.

Once Hamath could call her Orontes valley home her own; once she was free to come and go at will—but not now. Now her people were forced into subjugation, her hopes into exile.

If Israel would go from Hamath to "Gath of the Philistines" (via the southwestern branch of the Great Trunk Road), she would find a city-capital tottering on its last legs. Once Gath was great—the Home of the Philistine Giants (Goliath being the greatest of them all). Once Philistia so dominated God-chastened Israel, the Israelites were unable to forge tools (let alone weapons) without consent from their Levant Coast overseers. But over the years, Gath had diminished—Hazael of Syria took her captive, and Uzziah of Judah broke down her walls.

Once Gath also was great—but not now. Now she was on her way out. Soon she would waste away with no one to care. In time, only a handful of dirt-loving archeologists would dig her past.

Calneh, Hamath, Gath. Three cities from the past.

If Northern Israel would learn from their history, she might yet write *The Compleat Guide to Survival as a Middle East Nation.* But if not . . .

If she could not be bothered with the lessons of history—

history would one day overtake her, shove her aside and leave her nothing more than a footnote in a young teen's book.

THE DOUBLE STANDARD

"You only have I chosen from all the nations of the earth. Therefore it is you whom I will punish for all your wrongdoings" (Amos 3:2, Phillips).

A mother lovingly reassures her questioning child. "No, God would never allow anything to happen to this country. This is a Christian land—a nation under God."

Amos was a lowly man, but not ignorant. A simple man, but not untaught. His documentation of historical event was faultless; *his facts came from an unimpeachable source.* His interpretation of historical fact was impeccable; *his point of view was that of the Great Historian Himself.*

Unlike many of the ancient-world "historians" who dutifully chronicled the press releases of their larger-than-life kings in epic scenes of full-blown fantasy, Amos penned the historical picture in fine-lined, "warts and all" truth. His depiction of history—past, present and future—was precisely drawn, exact down to the final "This is it" period.

Not only that. Amos was not subject to the bondage humanity imposes upon even the greatest of historians. He was not liable to the limits within which finite man must observe and record. For try as a man may to aim after historical truth, he is still human. He has his own subjective self, his own background bias to contend with. And seek as a man may after objectivity, he is still fallible—by a slight shift of emphasis, a quote misused, a blurring of detail, a selectivity error he may unwittingly distort his painstakingly researched facts beyond recognition.

Furthermore, what single historian ever has free access to *all* the facts in any given event, *all* the written exchanges, *all* the tapes, *all* the closed-door secrets of the heart? What man knows (let alone is able to rightly interpret) the inner life of the many and varied actors that people the pages of history? What man knows the motivation that prompts their acts, the satanic forces at work, the pressures, the alternatives?

Above and beyond all this, what man is able to discern the hand of the King of Heaven and Earth as He controls the reigns of government? What man has in view the behind-the-scene working of the Sovereign God as He raises up one earthly rule and puts down another (without violating the free will of either)?

Left to himself, no historian, however great, is sufficient for these things. Of necessity he is limited to the light he has, the knowledge he possesses. Beyond that he cannot go.

Amos, on the other hand, was not limited to himself. At his disposal was the complete print-out of Almighty God. The eternal knowledge of the omnipotent, omniscient and omnipresent God was in his possession. He spoke not for himself but for God.

Therefore, for a nation such as Israel to cut any class Amos might conduct in the *Lessons of History* was folly. Indeed, for any nation, in any age, to ignore the divinely given truths Amos sets forth as to *what has happened, what is happening and what will happen*—is the height of folly.

It is a "sign of the times." A further fruit of a nation hellbent on its way up—and out.

As a man of God, Amos was refreshingly unsophisticated in his ways; yet he was by no means naive. The inner workings of the Capitol Hill set—the court intrigue, the power politics maze, the hand-holding, back-scratching, knee-scraping antics of the respected leaders of the foremost nation were not for him. He had a brand of political diplomacy all his own.

First, he gained the rapt attention of the assemblage at Bethel by proclaiming God's judgment on Israel's enemies, beginning with those most distant and moving in to those next door. Then, when his audience was at ease, lined up before him like sitting ducks—he mentioned their name.

Israel, too, would come under the just judgment of God.

But first, their enemies—those "gentile dogs" whose very presence put a blight on the neighborhood; those immoral pagans whose behaviour was an affront to the ethical standards of God—they would be meted out punishment fit for their crimes . . .

For crimes against humanity, Damascus would be punished.
For crimes against humanity, Philistia would be punished.
For crimes against humanity, Phoenicia would be punished.

Circling high over the heads of the men of Israel, the wrecking-ball judgments of God dead-centered, let loose and moved on—leaving a trail of desolation in their wake.

For crimes against humanity, Edom would be punished.
For crimes against humanity, Ammon would be punished.
For crimes against humanity, Moab would be punished.

Without warning Amos dead-centered on Israel. The whole family, both Ephraim and Judah, was next for demolition.

For crimes against humanity, Israel would be punished. For savage cruelty, for threshing the poor until they all but perished, for reducing her people to human bondage, for tossing her Great Unwashed on the dunghill of slavery, for breaking her covenants, for stifling natural affection with unrighteous "brotherly love," for nursing anger, for cherishing wrath, for entertaining revenge, for unspeakable acts of sadism, perversion and violence—Israel would pay dearly.

There would be no double standard, no favored nation treatment. By order of the Lord God, Israel would fall.

Nor was that all.

For crimes against God, Israel would be doubly punished. Whereas the heathen "who had never heard" were sinning against unaided conscience, Israel had full knowledge of what she was doing. Whereas the pagans reared "no gods" in a vain attempt to fill the empty throne of their hearts, Israel dethroned the living God to make room for substitute-rivals.

Thus, for every performance of the Jeroboam Follies, for religious "much ado" about nothings, for hypocritical worship "in the Name of God," for rejecting the Word of God, for following the statutes of Omri and Ahab, for the folly of "no return" and for the parting of the ways—Israel would pay dearly.

By order of the Lord God, the house of Israel would be shaken among all nations as grain is shaken in a sieve.

Too late Israel would learn that all nations of the earth are responsible to God, whether they acknowledge Him or not; whether they are a "nation under God" or not.

Too late Israel would learn that if there is any "double standard" with God, it is this: "To whom much is given, much will be required."

Therefore, a nation that convenants with God at its inception is not only singularly privileged: it is *doubly* accountable.

THE SECURITY OF FOOLS

"All those who say, 'Disaster will never touch us and can never threaten our security,' Shall be killed with the sword " (Amos 9:10, Phillips).

A late-show celebrity avers: "Nothing can happen here. Disaster will never touch us. We are secure."
With this, the lights go out, security blankets are piled high and America dreams on, and on . . .

When Josiah, king of Judah, heard the reading of the law of God, he wept before the Lord. The rude awakening, the sudden awareness of his nation's accountability to the Holy One in their midst, was not easy for any man to take. Not even a godly leader.

Josiah wept and led his people back to God. The folly of "no return" was not for him, nor for his people. Consequently, revival fires swept throughout the Southern Kingdom: purifying the hearts of individual believers, purging the land of false gods and extending the period of divine grace. All his days Judah-Israel was safe, secured by the hand of Almighty God.

Not so, Ephraim-Israel.

When Amos thundered the outraged holiness of a righteous God, the Northern Kingdom shrugged. "Disaster will never touch us."

When the trouble-in-the-city alarm sounded, Ms. Samaria yawned and rolled over, turned off the alarm and stretched herself luxuriously, pulled the curtain on reality and closed her eyes to divine light, snuggled under the security blankets piled high on her ivory couch—and went back to sleep.

And so to dream . . .
All is well. Nothing has changed. Tomorrow will be even as today. Are we not the chosen people of God? The Foremost Nation? Disaster and calamity can never threaten our security.

We are a good people. We are religious; our *Temple Progress Reports* will verify that. We are upright; there is no iniquity in us that would be called sin. Our godly beginnings, our sacred heritage, our present prosperity, our obvious privileges—all these attest to our favored nation standing before God.

We are unique, a law unto ourselves. Therefore, we are exempt from the laws of cause-and-effect. We are not subject to divine judgment, nor will we give account in the day of reckoning. We are above the laws of history; they do not apply to us. Calneh might fall; Hamath might go into captivity; Philistine Gath might disappear from the face of the earth, but not our great nation.

We will live forever.

Dream on, Ephraim-Israel. Dream on . . .

THE GRACE PERIOD

"It may be that the LORD God of hosts will be gracious unto the remnant of Joseph" (Amos 5:15b).

WHAT DO YOU SEE?
THE GRACE GOD
THE THRONE OF GRACE
AMAZING GRACE
THE GRACE PERIOD

WHAT DO YOU SEE?

"This is what the Lord God showed me in a vision . . ." (Amos 7:1a, TLB).

Look around, America. What do you see?

Amos saw the truth about Israel . . .
Amos saw massive-stroke judgments ahead should Israel refuse to return to the Lord; disasters, calamitous "acts of God" in the offing should Israel persist in the folly of "no return."

In a God-given prophetic vision, Amos saw swarming locusts descend *en masse* upon the slumbering land, devouring, consuming, leaving no remnant of the tender green growth sprouting up after the king's mowing. He saw locusts *formed by God* stripping the fields bare, divesting the land like avenging adversaries.

Alarmed at the grievous sight, Amos rushed to Israel's side. "O Lord, forgive, what will Jacob be after this? He is so small." At this the Lord relented and stayed His hand of judgment.

"It shall not be."

"It shall not be." How long would the Lord withhold impending judgment from the errant land?

Amos had no way of knowing.

THE GRACE GOD

"It may be that the LORD God of hosts will be gracious unto the remnant of Joseph" (Amos 5:15b).

"America, America, God shed His grace on thee . . ."

The "no gods" Israel so eagerly pursued were cruel in the extreme. They were brutal, bloodthirsty tyrants. Sadistic monsters that only a die-hard masochist could love and adore.

They were *nothing gods,* in every sense of the word. Empty headed and empty hearted. Devoid of understanding and compassion, without capacity for loving-kindness and forgiveness, bereft of mercy and grace.

To a god, they were merci*less* and grace*less,* and as for caring —they couldn't care less about the house of Israel.

Actually, Israel was not alone in embracing despotic deities. Nor were the golden calves (for which she cold-shouldered the living God) her only folly. Like most of the peoples of the ancient world, she shared her religious bed and board indiscriminately with all comers—god-swapping with heathen neighbors on a sort of early day "try it, you'll like it" exchange basis.

Aside from her golden calves (which Ephraim-Israel apparently kept for herself as national gods), the great god Baal was her principal male deity. Baal (the husband of the land, the lord or owner of the ground) at various times and in various places doubled as *the War God, the Fertility God, the Rain God, the Storm God, the God of the Sky, the Lord of the Gods, the King of Heaven and the Creator of Mankind.*

109

Moreover, Baal (alias Molech, Moloch, Bel, Belus, Baal-zebub Lord of Flies, Baal-Peor, Balal-Melkart, etc.) was the Number One god of Israel's pantheon—adopted and adapted from the Canaanites and the Phoenicians (via Tyre born-and-bred Jezebel) and modified to suit Israel's altered lifestyle patterns.

At Baal's side was his consort, Asherah, Israel's principal female deity. By any other name (Astarte, Ashtart, Ashtaroth, Ashtoreth, Baalath and Ishtar) she was still essentially the same: *the Mother God, the Mother of the Gods, the Queen of Heaven, the Moon Goddess and the Fertility Goddess.*

It was in honor of this infamous patroness of sex that the people of Israel devotedly performed lustful, licentious "acts of worship" consecrated to her ladyship's holy name.

Now Israel had to pay dearly to worship at the shrine of such erotic overlords. For Baal and Asherah, along with their lesser-lord entourage—*El, the (Ugarit) Father God, and Anath, the incestuous Warrior Goddess sister-mistress of Baal,* as well as related local deities (the Baalim) and regional gods of labor, agriculture, health, economy and welfare—didn't come cheap. They had to be approached with fear and trepidation.

Who would dare arouse their divine displeasure? Who would risk provoking their vindictive wrath?

Who could weather the full force of their abrupt mood changes? Who could ride out the storm of their capricious whims?

Who could chance the fall from their good graces?

Obviously, no one.

So, not unlike highly organized syndicate bosses, these infamous gangster-gods were to be appeased by the masses; systematically paid off for divine protection.

For demon-inspired prognostication of the future, their palms were crossed with costly gifts and offerings; for atonement for the past, their altars were drenched with blood.

For present favors, their going rate was whatever the current god-exchange would bring in the way of ecclesiastical bribes: choice wine and oil, first fruits of the land and firstlings of the flock; sacrifical feasts, prayers, vows, libations, purifications and ordeals by fire; the foreskin of a little child (as commutation for his life); the ritualistic leapings of demon-possessed, self-lacerating priests; violent, howling group sex orgies, or, if the situation were desperate enough (if there were overwhelming grief or sorrow, as in a national calamity), the supreme sacrifice was in order.

A human being (preferably not oneself) was ceremoniously sacrificed as a burnt offering to the great god Baal. A slave, a child, a first born son was given to the implacable Baal of the Heavens—cremated alive on Baal's furnace-heated image.

"O Baal, hear us! O Baal, answer us!"

But there was no voice; no one answered . . .
No one heeded. No one cared.

How different is the living God, the listening God, the loving God, the Grace God . . .

O ISRAEL, return unto the LORD thy God; for thou hast fallen by thine iniquity . . . Take with you words, and turn to the LORD: say unto Him, Take away all iniquity, and receive us graciously. . . .

It may be that the LORD God of hosts will be gracious unto the remnant of Joseph . . . for the LORD is merciful and gracious, slow to anger and plenteous in mercy. He will not always chide; neither will He keep His anger forever.

THE THRONE OF GRACE

"Then I said, 'O Lord God, please forgive your people! Don't send them this plague!'" (Amos 7:2a, TLB).

Pray, America, pray. It may be that the Lord your God will yet be gracious to your great nation.

In a second God-given prophetic vision, Amos saw a great fire advance upon the slumbering land; a supernatural fire *summoned by God* to lick up all moisture, consume tinder-dry fields of grain and torch the sky with flames. He saw a national conflagration raging out of control, destroying the fruit of all Israel's labor, wasting the land like a conquering enemy host.
Alarmed at the grievous sight, Amos rushed to Israel's side. "O Lord God, forgive; what will Jacob be after this?"
Then the Lord relented and stayed His fiery judgment.
"This also shall not be."

"This also shall not be." How long would the Lord withhold just judgment from the truant land? How long would the Throne of Grace grant audience to the prayers of men?

Amos had no way of knowing. He would intercede for Israel as long as he could, but then. . . .

When Amos saw the truth about Israel, he did not despair; for at the same time, he saw the truth about Israel's God—the Grace God in her midst.

Like the other prophets of old, Amos saw the Lord God high and lifted up. By faith, he lifted his eyes to behold a God of infinite grandeur and vastness—a God above and beyond His creation, incomparable, immeasurable, unlimited in power—a God of surpassing magnitude, whose glory cannot be encompassed . . .

"For, lo, he that formeth the mountains, and createth the wind, and declareth unto man what is his thought, that maketh the morning darkness, and treadeth upon the high places of the earth, the LORD, the God of hosts is his name."

Yet for all this great glory, Amos saw *as well* a God graciously inclined toward His creation. A God eager to be sought after by mankind, to be found. "Seek ye me, and ye shall live."

In this *far yet near* view of God, Amos was not alone. The prophet Isaiah visioned the Lord sitting upon a throne, high and lifted up; he heard the seraphim of heaven call one to another, "Holy, holy, holy is the LORD of hosts: the whole earth is full of his glory." Isaiah was awe-stricken. "My eyes have seen the King, the LORD of hosts!"

Yet, for all his lofty view of the Majesty on high, Isaiah saw *as well* a God concerned with the welfare of His creation; a God inviting men to approach, communicate and enter into right relationship with Him.

"Come now, and let us reason together," saith the LORD: "Though your sins be as scarlet, they shall be as white as snow; though they be red like crimson, they shall be as wool."

Far above, yet close at hand. This was the view also given the prophet Hosea. The solitary splendor of the Sovereign God, "There is no saviour beside me . . ." offset by the tender compassion of the love of God for Israel. "I will court her again . . . I will heal their backsliding, I will love them freely. . . ."

Such gentle, intimate words were entrusted to Hosea's care: "When Israel was a child, then I loved him. It was I who taught

Ephraim to walk, picking them up in my arms. Yet they never knew that it was I who healed their bruises. . . .

"Oh Israel, how well I remember those first delightful days when I led you through the wilderness! How refreshing was your love. How satisfying . . . but then you deserted Me for Baal-Peor, to give yourselves to other gods. . . .

"How can I give you up, O Ephraim! My heart recoils within me, my compassion grows warm and tender.

"Come home, Israel, come home to the LORD your God!"

The LORD your God.

It was to this God the prophets turned in their country's darkest hours. This "gracious and compassionate, long-suffering and ever constant, always ready to repent of the threatened evil" God the prophet Joel saw bending over the land in love. This eager-to-be-entreated God the prophet Micah approached with such confidence. "I will look unto the LORD; I will wait for the God of my salvation: my God will hear me . . . He will turn again, he will have compassion upon us; he will subdue our iniquities . . . because he delighteth in mercy."

It was to this God *enthroned in grace*, that Amos came on Israel's behalf. Like the prophet Habakkuk, he came in awe, in reverent fear. "The LORD is in his holy temple: let all the earth keep silence before him."

He stood as though on holy ground, yet he did not grovel in the dirt or abase himself as did the idolators before Baal. Instead, he came with holy boldness!

"O LORD, forgive. What will Jacob be after this?"

Thus, like the true prophet he was, Amos stood in the gap between Israel and her God. Before the people, he was an ambassador for God, an "advisory signboard," a voiceprint. But before God, he was a voice lifted on behalf of the sinning people.

His voice was heard, his intercession was effectual and his power in prayer prevailed—not because of who he was, but because it was a *Throne of Grace* to which he came. It was not the merit of his person, nor the eloquence of his prayer, but the *worthiness of the One upon the throne* that availed. As Daniel would pray, "O LORD . . . we do not present our supplications before thee for our righteousness, but for thy great mercies. . . ."

"*For thy great mercies . . .*" the prophets stormed the battlements of heaven. Their prayer life on behalf of their country was vital and alive, their prayers earnest and impassioned. "The effectual fervent prayer of a righteous man availeth much."

"For thy great mercies . . ." the prophets locked horns with the problems of the nation and threshed them out before the Lord. With full knowledge of the revealed will of God, the lessons of history and the current "what is happening" scene, they daily presented to the Lord a prayer agenda designed to enable Him to bless their country by turning the people from their iniquities.

Before the Throne of Grace, they laid supplications, prayers, intercessions and giving of thanks. They prayed for kings and those that were in authority, that the people might lead a quiet and peaceable life in all godliness and honesty.

They prayed about the burning issues of the day: matters of national policy, social ills, foreign affairs, international commitment, corruption in high places, crime in the streets, economics, drought, plague, cold wars, hot wars and no-win wars.

They knew their place and stood their ground. They were persistent, but never presumptuous; impassioned, but never impertinent. They pressed the promises of God to the "n"th degree: "Thou has said . . ." but never exceeded the boundaries of the Word of God. At all times, they stayed on praying ground. Humble, expectant and fearless before the throne.

But they were not enough!

Without the undergirding prayers of the people, even the prophets could not stem the rising tide of evil threatening to engulf the land. Without the solid prayer support of the God-fearing minority, the nation would be swept away.

If the "prophet sharing" believers would not pray for their country, they would soon have no country to pray for!

But if they would pray . . .

If the faithful few of Amos' day would come to know God through His Word (as did the prophets); if they would take Him at His Word: "If my people, which are called by my name, shall humble themselves, and pray, and seek my face, and turn from their wicked ways . . ." then the Lord would heal their land.

Then the people of God would bequeath to their children one of the most priceless gifts one generation can bestow upon another—a *legacy of prayer-residuals* left in trust before the Everlasting Throne.

AMAZING GRACE

"Then the Lord relented, and the Lord said, 'This shall not be'"
(Amos 7:3, Phillips).

*America, America. Through "many dangers, toils and
snares," you have already come. . . .*

By the time Amos made the scene at Bethel, Ephraim-Israel
had come through many dangers, toils and snares. The struggles
of her early pioneer days were far behind; the century-and-a-
half mark as an independent nation had been rounded in great
style, and the years of her bicentennial were at hand.

It was grace that brought her safe thus far . . . grace alone.
Pure grace. Exceeding grace. Amazing grace.

It was grace, pure grace, that invited Amos to pray on Israel's
behalf, that opened his eyes to the truth about Israel, led him to
plead for national forgiveness while the land could yet be spared
and answered his cry before the judgment fell.

It was grace that gladly relented the called-for massive-stroke
chastening, that instantly aborted the plan, altered the course of
divine policy from wrath to mercy and gave yet another day for
Israel to repent and return to the LORD her God.

It was grace that transformed prayer into divine action. . . .

It was grace that gave audience to the solitary prayer of the
prophet Elijah, that sent healing, drought-ending showers
upon Israel in answer to that righteous man's fervent cry.

It was grace that answered the collective prayers of the God-
fearing minority of the land, that granted the requests of the
faithful few as they took their stand on praying ground and made
up the hedge between their country and their God.

It was grace that led them to identify openly and honestly with
their sinning people, to share their common cause, and to pray
earnestly and often that God would guide the course of their
nation, rule and overrule on matters of state, raise up men of
honor and good conscience and move or remove those in places
of authority.

It was grace that enabled "my people" to render unto God,
and to their country, the things due.

It was grace, exceeding grace, that remembered Israel's

forefathers and continued to honor them before the throne.

It was grace that exceeded the bounds of time and place in the desperate down-to-the-last-ten chariots reign of King Jehoahaz and kept the judging hand of God from destroying the land or casting them "from His presence as yet." The LORD was gracious and compassionate and had respect for that ungodly generation, not because of who they were, but because of His covenant made generations before with Abraham, Isaac and Jacob.

It was grace that honored the faith-filled, founding-father prayers of these godly men by showering residual blessings upon the land for generations to come.

But more than pure grace and more than exceeding grace, *it was amazing grace* that kept Israel going from day to day.

It was grace independent of prayer, grace nonreliant on covenants with man, grace without reference to human conduct or affairs, that brought Israel along year after year.

It was amazing grace: grace for no earthly reason, grace dependent upon the heavenly Father alone.

It was amazing grace that gave Israel another dawn.

It was amazing grace that gave Israel freedom to sing hymns to the rising sun, to prostrate herself before cosmic deities and to squander her national resources on ecological gods.

It was amazing grace that gave Israel liberty to dissipate her love under every green tree, to fritter away her life on pillow-strewn ivory couches and to dream on and on. . . .

It was amazing grace that entered into Israel's history without being invited; that raised up the administrative genius, Jeroboam II, to lead the nation to foremost prominence; that perpetuated the kingdom in spite of corruption on Capitol Hill, glaring mistakes made by government leaders and unholy alliances signed into being at the conference table.

It was amazing grace that rescued Israel from calamities of her own making, that interposed divine "pluck out" deliverances in impossible situations, intervened between cause-and-effect, circumvented the natural laws of sow and reap and put the day of reckoning on hold.

It was amazing grace that knew Israel's frame and remembered she was dust, that was touched with the feeling of her infirmities and pitied her as a father pities his children.

THE GRACE PERIOD

"Then I said, 'Oh Lord God, please don't do it. If you turn against them, what hope is there? For Israel is so small!'" (Amos 7:5, TLB).

How long, America? How long?

The prayer Amos offered on Israel's behalf was anything but eloquent. It made no attempt to laud Israel's praises or call attention to the land's inherent worth as a "nation under God" or its great works as a benefactor of mankind.

Rather, the intercessory prayer of Amos was a humble, yet forceful appeal for grace. An appeal for divine pardon for a flagrantly sinful nation, forgiveness for an unrepentant people and mercy for a nation "so small" it would collapse if God were to withdraw His gracious life-support systems.

It was a bold prayer, a direct thrust to the tender heart of a Father grieving over His beloved son—and it worked.

God was impressed, even if Israel was not.

In itself, the fact that (even under Jeroboam II) Israel was still comparatively small geographically was of little consequence. God had never intended His people to become great empire builders and throw their corporate weight around. Rather, they were called to be a showcase nation—to witness to His glory and give evidence of His grace. For this, little more than a thumb's width on a back-of-the-Bible map was needed.

No. The "so small" condition that threatened the very life expectancy of Ephraim-Israel was not so much his size as his character (or lack of it). For he was not just a "prodigal son," a one-time runaway blowing his inheritance on profligate living, he was an "unwise son"—a stubborn, resisting babe-in-the-womb refusing to face the light of day and grow up.

In this, Israel was unwise. For the Lord "disciplines him whom He loves and chastises every son whom He receives."

The Lord is balanced in Himself, well-adjusted in His perfect essence. He is neither a sentimental fool nor a cruel despotic deity. In His goodness, He is severe; in His graciousness, He chastens. And in His loving-kindness, He woodsheds "unwise sons."

His love knows no limits, *but His leniency does.*

How long would the grace period last for Ephraim-Israel?
How long would the grace appeal, "He is so small," stay God's uplifted hand of judgment?
How long would God relent and say, "It shall not be"?

Amos would soon know.

THE FINAL APPEAL

"Seek the Lord and live, or else . . ." (Amos 5:6a, TLB).

THE PLUMB LINE
THE DEATH HOUSE
THE GOD OF HOSTS
NO HIDING PLACE
THE FINAL APPEAL

THE PLUMB LINE

"Behold, the Lord stood upon a wall made by a plumb line, with a plumb line in his hand" (Amos 7:7).

Line upon line, a nation builds its future . . .

In a third God-given prophetic vision, Amos saw a wall made with a plumb line, a vertical wall of Israel's own building. Upon the wall stood the Lord Himself, plumb line in hand.

"Amos, what do you see?" asked the Lord.
Amos answered, "A plumb line."
Then the Lord said, "I will set a plumb line in the midst of my people Israel: I will not again pass by them. . .
"I will not relent again."

At this, Amos was silent. There was nothing more to be said. The lines were drawn; the door to intercessory prayer was closed.
The grace period had all but expired.

120

When the cornerstone of the Northern Kingdom of Israel was laid (circa 931 B.C.), God promised Jeroboam I a "sure house." A present rule over all his soul desired and an ongoing dynasty would be his upon recognition of the God of Israel as the one fixed authority, the absolute ruler over the land.

To the kingdom was given a master plan for building national integrity—a basic structural guide securing right standing before God. If the divine blueprint were followed, the weight of years would not crush the "nation under God," nor would the winds of change huff and puff and blow the house down.

From the onset, the high standards of God were available for Israel's use. At the nation's disposal was the whole body of truth: the uprights of the Word of God, the ethics of the divine nature, the value system of eternal verities and the straight-down-the-line "This is it" plumb bobs—the commandments.

From the ten monumental *Code for Living* pillars outlined on Mount Sinai, through the person-to-person dovetailing detailed in the *Book of Leviticus,* there was a single measuring line for the nation: the immutable, unalterable righteousness of God.

The plumb line rule would be at once Israel's blessing and cursing. If the people aligned with its fixed perpendicular, correcting their deviations and mistakes as they went along, the nation would be solid and substantial; if not, it would give way under stress. If they used the plumb of God as an objective guide in matters of decency, honor, morality and excellence, the nation would rise to great heights; if not, it would fall.

It would not be their perfection of person that would make the nation great, but their willingness to build *line upon line* with God.

This Israel would not do.

So over the years the house that Israel built was of her own rule, not God's; her own eased-out relativity codes, not God's rigidly righteous standards. Hence nothing jibed; nothing trued. *The whole nation was out of plumb!*

Indeed, by the reign of Jeroboam II, the house of Israel resembled a structural engineer's nightmare—an ivory-towered horror swaying with the changing winds of public opinion, bending to the mood of the moment, spacing out and settling on its "we the people" lees.

"Amos, what do you see?" asked the Lord.

121

Amos answered, "A plumb line."

A plumb line . . . *and a bowing wall* spiderwebbed with jagged cracks bespeaking the nation's structural integrity damage and foretelling its future.

A plumb line . . . *and a tottering wall* caving in of its own weight and subject to imminent collapse.

A plumb line . . . *and a jerry-built house*, the end result of flexible standards, cheap materials, shoddy workmanship and haphazard "every man a rule unto himself" ways.

A plumb line . . . *and a house of cards* put together by two-faced kings and queens; an insubstantial edifice held in place by ornamental latticework, ivory panels, vermilion paint . . . and grace.

THE DEATH HOUSE

"Because I will do this unto thee, prepare to meet thy God, O Israel!" (Amos 4:12b).

> *"I tremble for my country when I reflect that God is just."*
> *(Thomas Jefferson)*

"Amos, what do you see?" asked the Lord.
Amos answered, "A plumb line."

A plumb line . . . *and a Tower of Babel,* a public nuisance unfit for occupancy, a dangerous menace to society, a demolition project in the making.

Ephraim would be desolate in the day of rebuke. The plumb line so graciously given would no longer bless, but curse. Once the line that the builders rejected descended from the hand of the Lord, the degree of Israel's deviation from the divine norm would be revealed. The grace period would come to an end; condemnation proceedings would begin.

By order of the Lord, the once-great nation would be measured for destruction, the wrecking ball readied for demolition. "The high places of Isaac shall be desolate, and the sanctuaries of Israel shall be laid waste. . . .

"I will not pass by and spare them any more."

"Because I will do this unto thee, prepare to meet thy God, O Israel!"

Israel would go to meet his Maker unprepared. Having refused to return to the Throne of Grace, he would appear before the Judgment Bar without a redeeming feature.

He would be without hope. Without a prayer, without a rag of excuse. His substitute-rival righteousness threads would be found full of holes; he would be exposed, naked and open unto the eyes of Him with Whom he had to do. He would have no covering from the gaze of the Judge upon the bench, no ecclesiastical garb, no dream world scrim, no fifth amendment to hide behind.

He would be without representation. *If a man sins against the Lord, who can intercede for him?* No storefront attorney would rush to his aid; no public defender would present his case. His would be a *nonsuit:* one having no triable issue.

He would be without a plea. Speechless. He would stand before the tribunal of the Almighty God, hushed and guilty; his proud lips silenced, his "I was framed," stillborn.

For multiple crimes against humanity, for multiple crimes against God, Israel would be charged before the court. For light rejected, for standards lowered, for warnings ignored, for chastening unheeded, for sins of commission, of omission: the nation would be prosecuted to the full.

No objection would be raised, no challenge made. *Exhibit A: the house that Israel built* would still every voice.

Unlike the uneven courts of the land, the high court of heaven would permit no respect for persons. Rich man, poor man, beggar man, thief—all would receive impartial judgment.

Unlike the circus atmosphere of Israel's legal system, the sideshow tricks, the twisting, the turning, the divine proceedings would be handled with dignity and reserve.

Unlike the presiding judges of Israel's bench, their admission of false testimony and perjured witnesses, their acceptance of bribes, the Judge on Israel's case would be above reproach.

The judgment would be just; the death penalty handed down. The date of execution set on God's calendar.

The judgment would be irreversible. The case, closed. "I will not revoke the judgment. I will not relent again."

Once decreed, the sentence would stand. There would be no appeal. No retrial. No reopening of the case for the entrance of further evidence. No mistrial declared. No reverse opinion.

The death penalty would not be considered cruel and unusual punishment. Capital punishment would not be banished; death row would not be disbanded. In no way would Israel get home free.

Overnight, *the house that Israel built* would become a death house, a maximum security facility, a prison of his own making. There Israel would remain until the woeful day, with no parole, no reprieve, no stay of execution.

As a prisoner of his own folly, Israel would live out his days serving time—going through the motions of an automatic existence, eating, sleeping, putting one foot down, then the next—awaiting the last day, the final meal, the long walk.

Israel's waning days as a nation would be lived "under the gun." Watchmen would mark his every move; guards would discover his every hiding place. There would be none to help, no way of escape. The streets of Samaria would become chill, dank corridors, the grand houses on Samaria's heights tiered cellblocks. In every courtyard would be heard the cry, "Alas! Alas!"

Long before the evil day, the dying process would set in. Day by day, the preexecution deterioration of the nation would take its deadly toll. As a prisoner condemned, Israel would "die behind the walls." His privilege card as a "nation under God" would be taken from him. His freedoms, rights and power of self-determination would be lost. Traumatic emotional and mental experiences would fragment his personality; in-stir violence would pen his final days with blood.

Then would come the end.

THE GOD OF HOSTS

"For lo, he who forms the mountains, and creates the wind, and declares to man what is his thought; who makes the morning darkness, and treads on the heights of the earth—the Lord, the God of hosts, is his name!" (Amos 4:13, RSV).

The fool says, "There is no God."

O Israel, prepare to meet thy God!

He it is that forms the mountains and creates the wind. . . . He made the earth by His power and established the world by

His wisdom. He stretched out the heavens by His discretion.

He gave the sun for a light by day and the ordinances of the moon and of the stars for a light by night; he weighed the mountains in scales and the hills in a balance. He divided the sea; He measured the waters in the hollow of His hand.

The Lord, the God of hosts, is His name.

He rebukes the sea and makes it dry; He touches the land and it melts, and all that dwell therein mourn. The mountains quake at Him; the hills melt, and the earth is burned at His presence. He has His way in the whirlwind and in the storm. . . .

O Israel, if you sow the wind, shall you not reap the whirlwind? Shall you not be as the chaff that is driven with the whirlwind out of the floor? Shall not the whirlwind of His wrath blow you away as stubble?

He declares unto man what is his thought. . . .

His eyes behold, His eyelids try, the children of men.

From the place of His habitation He looks upon all the inhabitants of the earth. He searches all hearts and understands all the imaginations of the thoughts. He knows the secrets of the heart.

His Word is a discerner of the thoughts and intents of the heart, a discloser of motivations, of purposes. . . .

O Israel, can you hide yourself in secret places that He shall not see you? Does He not fill heaven and earth? Has He not searched and known your thoughts afar off? Are not His judgments as the light that goes forth?

He makes the morning darkness and treads upon the high places of the earth. . . .

The Lord is a God of knowledge; by Him actions are weighed. His judgment is according to truth; He will render to every man according to his deeds.

The Lord is slow to anger and great in power and will not at all acquit the wicked.

O Israel, shall not the Judge of all the earth do right? Shall mortal man be more just than God? Shall a man be more pure than his Maker?

The Lord is the King of Nations. . . .

All nations before Him are as nothing, and they are counted to Him less than nothing. Behold, the nations are as a drop in the bucket and are counted as the small dust of the balance.

He brings the princes to nothing; He makes the judges of the earth as vanity. Among all the wise men of the nations and all their kingdoms, there is none like unto Him.

The Lord is the true God; He is a living God and an everlasting King. At His wrath the earth shall tremble, and the nations shall not be able to abide His indignation.

He stands and measures the earth; He beholds and drives asunder the nations. He strides upon the high places of the earth; He puts away the wicked of the earth like dross. He trods down all them that err from His statutes. . . .

O Israel, is it not a fearful thing to fall into the hands of the living God? Can you stand before His indignation? Can you abide in the fierceness of His wrath?

The Lord, the God of hosts, is His name. . . .

He is the king of glory: the Lord strong and mighty, the Lord mighty in battle. The Commander of the Lord's hosts.

He it is that musters hosts for the battle, that marches through the land in indignation, that pours out the fierceness of His anger and strength of battle.

O Israel, having once led your armies into the land, is He not now able to lead them out again? To lead them out as captives to your enemies? As prisoners on that long walk beyond Damascus?

O proud ungodly nation . . .

When the plumb line of the Lord of the armies, the God of hosts, is set in your midst, what will be your chances?

NO HIDING PLACE

"I saw the Lord standing beside the altar . . ." (Amos 9:1a, TLB).

The fool says, "I'll take my chances."

In a further God-given prophetic vision, Amos saw the Lord standing beside the altar (presumedly the pagan altar at Bethel).

No longer was He forming locusts to plague Israel or summoning fire to purge the land; no longer was He measuring for off-plumb deviation or numbering the nation's days . . .

In this vision, the zero hour was at hand. The LORD, the God of hosts, was ordering the death of the nation.

Smash the tops of the pillars and shake the temple until the pillars crumble and the roof crashes down upon the people below. Though they run, they will not escape; they all will be killed.

Judgment would begin at the house of God (such as it was). Just as smashing overhead blows to the ornate pillars bracing the substitute-rival temple at Bethel would shatter the entire structure, so massive-stroke wrecking-ball judgments descending from God would level the Northern Kingdom of Israel.

The nation would fall in on itself.

Once the death house judgment on Israel was pronounced, what would be the nation's chances?

Israel could chance that the Judge of all the earth would not do right—that He might reconsider His verdict, make an exception in Israel's case or declare a mistrial because of some technicality, some fluke; at least, that He would find some loophole through which the nation could escape, *legally.*

Barring this, Israel could chance a bold approach and appeal his case himself. He could wheel up to the Judgment Bar on his bright and shiny "I am a victim of society" cycle and sing a little "I am so small" song for good measure (no court in the land could withstand such a pitiful plea).

Or, if not this, Israel could chance that the LORD, the God of hosts, was bluffing—that He didn't have the omnipotence called for to back up His threatened judgments or the high-above-all power to execute His death sentence decrees.

Once the wrecking-ball judgments against Israel began, what would be the nation's chances of escape?

Israel could chance that the fallout of God's wrath would not touch him if he stayed within the fortress walls of Samaria. Given ample warning of approaching danger, he could cancel a few appointments, dash across town to withdraw his gold ingots from the temple bank, round up his family and take up residence in his well-stocked subterranean storehouse. There he could sit, smug and defiant on his *Family Fallout Shelter* pad, until the sword of the Lord passed over.

Then he could emerge, untrammeled and free, to build a brave new world—according to his own plumb line measure.

If this didn't work, Israel could take his chances on the open road. Any time he chose to do so, he could throw a few things together, pack up his old lady and head for the hills.

He could follow the boldly marked *dashed-orange route* on the DIVISION OF HIGHWAYS trade route map or hit the lesser known, more scenic trails—the choice was his. Either way, he chanced a grand and glorious traffic jam—with tailgating stock, stalled campers, stranded dune-buggies and overheated drivers adding to the built-in disaster potential.

Nor were these all the available chances! If Israel took the main freeway to the Mediterranean beach towns (in an understandable effort to escape the divine heat wave), he chanced finding the westbound arteries so clogged he was boxed in to the number one lane; if he took the alternate by-paths (to escape the maddening crowd), he chanced being hemmed in by heavy military equipment or overrun by troops engaged in a disorderly retreat.

Moreover, if his exodus were on the Sabbath (heaven forbid), his chances diminished appreciably—he might get stuck behind a rubbernecking "Sabbath driver" who finally found himself *out there* and wasn't going to miss the sights, national emergency or no. Furthermore, he chanced finding no roadside rest areas, no call boxes, no PASSING LANE AHEAD signs and no Moses. And what would an exodus be without a Moses to direct traffic?

Now if Israel were his own wheelman (like the bloody King Jehu), there was always the chance he might escape the crush in a cloud of dust. Then he could turn up almost anywhere!

If he were religiously inclined, there was the chance he might find asylum at a monastic mountain retreat. There he could attempt a climb to heaven via "In the Name of God" apostate worship. And if he didn't quite make the grade on his own, there was still an off chance the Lord would snatch him up in a chariot of fire and transport him heavenward in a whirlwind (a la Elijah).

On the other hand, if he were more of a downhill racer type, Israel might varoom for the Mediterranean, get carried away and wind up on a voyage to the bottom of the sea (a la Jonah). Either way, Israel's chances of escape were not too promising.

Though they climb into the heavens, I will bring them down. Though they hide at the bottom of the ocean, I will send the sea-serpent after them to bite and destroy them.

Once the omnipotent sword of the Lord, the God of hosts, flashed throughout the land, what would be the nation's chances of survival?

Israel might chance finding a hiding place from the wrath of God on Mount Carmel—with its breathtaking views, grassy picnic grounds, rocky dells and wooded shoulders to cry upon.

Though they hide among the rocks at the top of Carmel, I will search them out and capture them.

If not Carmel's picturesque slopes, then a less inviting cave dweller's compromise might be reached. The accomodations might not be as plush as at the favorite watering hole, but . . .

Israel might chance hiding in the out-of-sight caves and caverns of the nearby Ephraim highlands—where Obadiah hid the prophets of God from the vengeful Jezebel; or Israel might chance reaching Michmash (eastward from Beth-aven), where frightened Israelites hid themselves in caves, in thickets, among the rocks, in high places and in pits—in the days of King Saul.

Israel might chance the cave of Adullam (in the rock-strewn Shephelah), where David and his outlaw band sought refuge from Saul, or En-Gadi, with its honeycombed limestone caves and subterranean springs. Israel might chance holing up in the cave-riddled cliffs of the Judean wilderness—where precipitous gorges and sheer escarpments would make his secret hiding place all but inaccessible to the military; or Israel might just roll up like a scroll in the Dead Sea caves—and take his chances on being well-preserved.

Prepare to meet your God in judgment, Israel! For you are dealing with the One who . . . crushes down the mountains underneath His feet: Jehovah, the Lord, the God of hosts, is His Name.

Beyond all this, what would be the nation's chances?

Israel could chance a flight of fancy. "Oh that I had wings like a dove! For then would I fly away, and be at rest."

Ephraim is a silly, witless dove . . . I throw My net over her and bring her down like a bird from the sky.

Israel could chance that exile would not be all that bad (better Red than dead). *Though they volunteer for exile, I will command the sword to kill them there. I will see to it that they receive evil and not good.*

Israel could chance taking his life. Perhaps the way of the grave would be the Great Escape.

Though they dig down to Sheol, I will reach down and pull them up.

Poor Israel! By this time, he would have blown his chances, and the whirlwind of God's wrath would have just begun!

THE FINAL APPEAL

"Seek the Lord and live . . ." (Amos 5:6a, TLB).

A man comes to the end of the road . . .

It is fitting that the final appeal made on behalf of the Northern Kingdom of Israel would be a grace appeal. "Seek the Lord and live. . . ."

It was not an appeal made by man to man, nor an appeal made by man to God. Rather, it was *an appeal made by God* . . . to the "no-return" nation.

The appeal was timely. For generations Israel had pursued a wrong-way collision course—persisting in off-ramp religious approaches, ignoring every God-given sig-alert, every "advisory signboard" warning. For generations Israel had maintained its determined course at the expense of honor and integrity . . .

For generations grace had pursued the wrong-way nation—warning, chastening, rumble stripping its way, hauling it out of scrapes with overhead "pluck outs," settling its claims out of divine court. For generations grace had kept it on the road—servicing its needs, fueling its tanks. But all in vain.

Now the grace period had all but expired.

No longer could grace transform prayer into divine action or intervene between cause-and-effect. No longer could grace keep Israel going from generation to generation.

When the two points converged—the termination of the wrong-way course and the expiration of the grace period—Israel would reach the point of no return as a nation.

Then would come the judgment. "Prepare to meet thy God, O Israel!" Justice would of necessity replace grace; wrath would replace mercy.

The divine court would convene. The Judge would pronounce just judgment. The death sentence would be exacted.

By order of the Lord, the nation would be no more.

But that time was not yet! The prophetic visions were not yet

reality . . .
    Nor need they ever be!

O Israel! Seek the Lord and live . . .

PROPHET GO HOME

"Then Amaziah sent orders to Amos, 'Get our of here, you prophet, you! Flee to the land of Judah and do your prophesying there!'" (Amos 7:12, TLB).

THE UNBEARABLE WORD
THE KING'S CHAPEL
A FAMINE ON THE LAND
A BASKET OF SUMMER FRUIT
A SONG OF GRIEF

THE UNBEARABLE WORD

"Amos has conspired . . . the land is not able to bear all his words" (Amos 7:10, RSV).

A man faithfully voiceprints the Word of God . . .

He speaks clearly, openly, honestly. He adds no inflection of his own, leaves no impression not of God.

He gives the whole counsel of God. Nothing more, nothing less. He rightly balances grace and judgment, goodness and severity, love and limits. He draws the line, drops the plumb bobs. "This is it."

*He warns of judgment to come; he shows the way of escape. He lifts the **Saviour-Redeemer-Messiah-King**. In the Name of the Lord Jesus Christ, he offers forgiveness for sin, grace for weakness, new life for old . . .*

He stands aside. His work is done.

The Word works on the consciousness of those listening.

It worms beneath the surface of their rationale, behind the front line of their defense.

Like a hammer it pounds on their subconscious, breaking in pieces rock-hard strongholds before the Lord. Like a mirror it reflects basic unreality patterns, showing out-of-line lifestyles, off-plumb deviations. Like a fire it burns; like a light it reveals the things hidden in darkness.

Like a sharp two-edged sword it pierces hearts, dividing asunder soul and spirit, joints and marrow. Without respect for persons it cuts to the quick—uncovering, exposing, laying bare. It leaves man devastated, naked and opened, vulnerable, without a cloak for sin.

The moment Amos finished voiceprinting the Word of God at Bethel, all hell broke loose. Satanic forces marshaled for combat; demon hosts mustered on the double. Principalities, dominions, unseen rulers of darkness, evil powers behind the Jeroboam throne—all assembled in full battle array.

The main event of the *Satan vs. Jehovah* conflict would not be contended in the fields, but before the altar at Bethel.

The future of Ephraim-Israel would be decided at the feet of the golden calf—here and now!

In one corner stood Amos: a lone champion for God. A David before Goliath; a rough-hewn rustic in an ecclesiastical wilderness. As a mighty lion in the forest roars his territorial rights, so he thundered the outraged holiness of a sovereign God (only such a voice could have been heard above the temple din).

"Seek the LORD and live, or else He will sweep like fire through Israel and consume her, and none of the idols in Bethel can put it out!"

In the other corner huddled the assembled leaders of the Northern Kingdom. In their hands lay the fate of the nation. The door to Israel's future hinged on their next move.

Their situation was grave. To a man, they were staggering, reeling from the succession of knock-down, drag-out messages delivered by Amos. Moreover, the whole land was disturbed, visibly shaken by the rain of hard-hitting words from God.

Time was running out, the hour of decision was at hand . . .

O Israel! The count has not yet begun! You are still on your feet! You can still throw in the towel and return to God! You can even now seek the LORD and live!

But no. In the end, it was a fast one-two direct from God that forced Israel to the either/or, return/no return ropes:

"The idol altars and temples of Israel will be destroyed; and I will destroy the dynasty of King Jeroboam by the sword."

Then and there, the nation made its decision. The Word of God that so pounded Israel round after round, causing it to tremble, roughing up its tidy image, putting its proud nose out of joint—the Word that went straight to the heart, laying open the inner man, leaving it exposed—the Word that sent Israel's temples throbbing, that left ears ringing as though an enraged lion were roaring in the midst—the Word that was so intolerable, so unbearable *must go.*

Amaziah, the high priest of the golden altar at Bethel, acted on behalf of the nation. To Jeroboam the king he sent a garbled account of the conflict, accusing Amos of plotting high treason. "The land is not able to bear all his words."

To Amos, he sent marching orders.

"Get out of here, you prophet, you! Flee to the land of Judah and do your prophesying there!

"Don't bother us here with your visions; not here in the capital, where the king's chapel is!"

Go away, you calamity howler, you! Peddle your religious wares elsewhere! Ply your eschatological trade in Judah if you will—but not here! There is no room for you (or your God) here!

Amos answered his opponent briefly. Boldly. A humble witness to his call from God, a simple reiteration of truth, a last warning of sure things to come—and he was done.

The confrontation was over. The bout decided.

The word spoken, the Unbearable Word, would one day judge the land.

THE KING'S CHAPEL

"But prophesy not again any more at Beth-el; for it is the king's chapel, and it is the king's court" (Amos 7:13).

A nation rejects the simple lines of the Word of God, and builds complex religious structures of its own.

136

If Amaziah, the high priest of the golden altar at Bethel, had not been an authorized spokesman for the Northern Kingdom, God would not have dealt with the nation as He did.

No single *prophet go home* decision would have been so final, so binding, if the high priest had spoken for himself alone.

But as it was, Amaziah was not alone in his substitute-rival religious corner.

All Israel threw its weight on his side.

Not only were satanic forces stirring him up and egging him on, not only were self-seeking rulers shadowboxing his every move and seconding his every word—the majority of the inhabitants of the land were lined up behind him and pushing hard.

Rich man, poor man, beggar man, thief, king, commoner, Samaria heights lounger, ghetto pavement sleeper—all went along with him gladly. All encouraged his fighting stance.

All reinforced his position. All strengthened his hand.

And where were the faithful few?

Where were the seconds who backed the prophet Amos?

Where were the fans of justice and fair play? The followers of straight-from-the-shoulder righteousness and truth?

Where were the prophet-sharing minority who gathered ringside to cheer God's champion on?

Where indeed!

For the most part, they were long gone.

On the way to the main event, they had been struck down at the union of Church and State.

A FAMINE ON THE LAND

"'The time is surely coming,' says the Lord God, 'when I will send a famine on the land—not a famine of bread and water, but of hearing the words of the Lord.'" (Amos 8:11, TLB).

When the young of the land hunger and thirst after righteousness, where will they be filled?

It is the Lord's delight to reveal Himself to man. It is His good pleasure to bridge the gap between heaven and earth and translate His thoughts into the languages of man.

It is His will that invites man to come and feast upon His Word; it is man's will that accepts or declines.

For those who dine to the fill, there is abundant life. For those who turn away, there is nothing.

It is the Lord's reserved right to refuse service to anyone who does not evidence a taste for the Word. It is His privilege to withhold the bread of life from anyone who casts it aside.

It is His will that withdraws the feast from anyone who rejects it, who finds it unappetizing and unpalatable.

Anyone who persistently refuses the Word will not be coaxed or forced to eat. His portion will simply be removed.

In no way would the Lord force-feed His "unwise son." The spiritual banquet Ephraim-Israel so disdainfully deemed unbearable would be removed. By order of the Lord, the sorest famine of all—*a spiritual famine sent by God*—would grip the land. The nation once entrusted with the ministry of the Word to heathen nations would itself become a mission field.

It would become a spiritual wasteland—not because it had never heard the Word of God, but because it had rejected it.

The drought called by the prophet Elijah, the Great Famine called in the days of Elisha would be as nothing compared to the drought-famine now called. It would devastate the land.

With truth restrained, error would run rampant. The ranks of the few still disseminating the true Word would be decimated. Those who survived the Church-State crunch would die off, with none to replace them. Scarcely a faithful reprover would remain; scarcely a voice would cry in the wilderness for God.

With no Amos to peg the way with "This is it" markers, Israel would become a trackless waste. With no established routes, no godly leaders to follow, Israel would become lost in a maze of uncertainties and ambiguities.

Where does a nation turn when it goes beyond God? Does it find comfort in its idols? Strength in its bureaucracies?

Shall it take a two-finger walk through the yellow pages to locate a local guru? Shall it consult a newspaper columnist? An astrological chart? Shall it follow a bumper sticker?

Shall it flip a coin?

The more Israel searched for relief from the spiritual drought condition, the more desperate the people would become.

As in a dry and thirsty land, they would stagger about aimlessly, longing for relief. As in a depressed valley, they would circle endlessly, locked in to trouble and tears.

There would be no abundance of life. The "cows of Bashan" would exceed the feed limit at the fancy watering places and still have leanness of soul. The men of Samaria would devour one another with dog-eat-dog ways and still hunger.

Sad to say, the young of the land would suffer the most from spiritual dehydration. "Beautiful girls and fine young men alike will grow faint and weary, thirsting for the Word of God."

As the spin-off of the "diminished seventh" generation, the young would be bored with the whole religious scene: the sacred cows, the "In the Name of God" hypocricies, the much ado. . . . But where would the young go? What would they do?

When the "beautiful girls and fine young men" hungered and thirsted after righteousness, where would they find it?

Surely not *out there* in suburbia. Out there they would find tract models of the "king's chapel and the king's court."

Out there every man would have his own substitute-rival religious "chapel," his own jerry-built "king's court." Every man would sit as king over his personally-designed religious complex, as absolute ruler over his self-styled high place.

Every man would have delusions of grandeur. He would be his own god, his own high priest, his own sovereign head from whom the plumb descends. "It seems to me, I feel that, I think . . ."

I think I will be like the Most High God!

Unimpressed, the young would move on. They would hear many words, but precious few from the Lord. A quote taken out of context, a verse torn to shreds by a trusted mentor . . .

In time, the young would become drifters—spiritual tumbleweeds without roots, without place. Their souls would be as empty of hope as a dried-up brook; their lives, as barren of promise as the goat-grazed, wind-and-rain-eroded Judean wilds.

Disillusioned and discouraged, they would wander far afield. A timid oasis of hope, a prospect of cooling shade for their fainting souls, an expanse of bright waters just ahead . . .

A shimmering mirage, a washed-out riverbed, a mound of colorless sand.

"Is this all there is?"

No, beautiful girls and fine young men, there is more. But how could you know?

A BASKET OF SUMMER FRUIT

"Thus the Lord God showed me: behold, a basket of summer fruit" (Amos 8:1, RSV).

A beautifully arranged basket of fruit graces the center of the dining table . . .

In a vision, the Lord showed Amos a basket of summer fruit.
"Amos, what do you see?" asked the Lord God. Amos answered, "A basket of summer fruit."
Then the Lord said, "The end has come upon my people Israel; I will never again pass by them."

In the days to come, Israel would have her heart's desire. She would be alone at last! No longer would the God of Israel be in her midst; no longer would He enter into her affairs unasked. *He would not even enter into the picture at all!*
Israel, herself, would be the whole show. Like a basket of beautifully arranged summer fruit, she would grace the Fertile Crescent dining table. Like a woven-wicker bowl chock-full of sun-ripened figs, rosy-cheeked pomegranates, dew-kissed olives and tender-skinned grapes, she would attract all eyes.
From every angle, the nation would be a thing of beauty—a breathtaking still life awaiting the artist's canvas.

Yet all the while, Israel would be dying. Dying by degrees. The moment she was severed from the vine that gave her life, the moment she was lopped from the tree that bore her with such grace, the death process would begin. Then slowly, steadily, surely, the end would come.
The root rebellion against the Lord that earlier cropped first fruits of inner-city strife and violence would reap an end-harvest of national disintegration. The laws of cause-and-effect that even now worked unchecked beneath the nation's beautifully polished facade would push it past its prime.

Israel would peak out as fruit *overripe for ruin!*

A cross-section cut of every segment of society—from the degenerative center at Bethel, on through the weakened fibers of morality, to widespread deterioration of integrity and

140

honor—would prove Israel to be a soft, pulpy, spoiling mass of decay.

The nation that so casually took corruption as a way of life would be found rotten to the core.

One day, the Assyrian flaying knife would skin the overripe summer fruit.

That day, the end would be at hand.

A SONG OF GRIEF

"Sadly I sing this song of grief for you, O Israel" (Amos 5:1, TLB).

Is it well with you, America? Is it well?

A prophet's lot is not a happy one.

Not only is he without honor in his own country and in his own house; not only is he targeted for a range of occupational hazards—contempt, derision, slander, abuse, ostracism, persecution, even death; not only is he denied a standing ovation and handed, instead, an invitation *to go home* . . .

In addition to all these things, the prophet bears a heavy load of personal grief and pain.

Consider his position. The true prophet stands between God and man. He is a link, a line of communication, a liason point between the two. He identifies with the heart of God, he identifies with the plight of man. He suffers the sorrows of both.

As one who tells forth the divine Word, he is naturally in the thick of the main-event struggles between God and man. If man will cross over to God's corner and identify with Him, the prophet is the most happy of men. But if not . . .

If not, the prophet is caught in the middle. He cannot withdraw from the fray; he is too deeply committed. If he did not care for both God and man, he would not be there. But he does care, and he is there—and he is torn between the two.

If the prophet of God were not so sensitive of soul, the rejection of God and His Word would not effect him so deeply.

If he could somehow stand apart and deliver a theological treatise on the spiritual causes for the fall of a nation—*without being touched personally;* if he could lead a discussion on the death agony of a once-great people—*without becoming drained emotionally;* if he could toll the death knell on a "nation under God"—*and then go out for a hot fudge sundae* . . . but he cannot. Therein lies his pain.

The prophet Amos was not the dispassionate dispenser of gloom he might seem. When the occasion demanded, he was righteously indignant with the people, yes; but never was he remote. Never did he keep them at arm's length or handle them as through a glove box. He was committed to God, and man, all the way.

He gave his all. And when his all was rejected, he gave the only thing he had left—his tears. His was not the loud wailing of the heathen, but the quiet weeping of the heart of God. For God, also, had given His all—and been rejected.

Only those who have loved, and lost, *and still love*—can fathom the depth of grief sounded in the lamentation:
Sadly I sing this song of grief for you, O Israel: Beautiful Israel lies broken and crushed upon the ground and cannot rise. No one will help her. She is left alone to die.

When Amos voiced the unrequited love of God to the sad measures of a funeral dirge—Israel couldn't have cared less.
When the roar of the lion ceased, and the gentle fallout of tears overtook the land—Israel couldn't have rejoiced more.
"Come, let us eat, drink and be merry!"

As though Amos had never graced the scene at Bethel, the Northern Kingdom went back to its chosen ways. As though God had never spoken, the people picked up the thread of their lives.
As in the days of Noah that were before the flood, they were eating and drinking, marrying and giving in marriage; as in the days of Lot (before the overthrow of Sodom), they bought, they sold, they planted, they built. . . .

In the temple at Bethel, the worshipers kissed the golden calf and sang noisy hymns to the heavy heart of God. In the shopping center by the East Gate, the scheming merchant princes rubbed their hands with glee (let the buyer beware).
In the city set upon a hill, Ms. Samaria laughed and danced in the streets. Like a ballerina poised atop a music box, like a bit of feminine fluff pirouetting on the points of her toes, she whirled

about her ivory setting to la-de-da songs of love. She dipped, she twirled; she revolved in endless variations on her chosen themes. She bowed, she curtsied; she lit her ornamental boudoir lamps, she kaleidoscoped a gaily-colored dream world out of free-spinning baubles, bangles and beads.

And why not?

Life was sweet in Israel. Honey dripped from beehived rocks. Terraced hillside vineyards flowed vintage wines. Well-laden olive trees ran rivers of oil. The sun shone, the rains came and the earth yielded a ground swell of rich crops and abundant harvests. Granaries overflowed, the economy flouished and prosperity spread over the land like a green bay tree.

But that was not all. Life was sweet, and the living was easy. Not since King Solomon's heyday had the Israel scene boasted such rich overlays of opulence and wealth. Throughout the length and breadth of Palestine, all a man might ever wish for was his for the taking.

The "good life" had come. Amos had gone.

"All is well! All is well!"

But all was not well with the backsliding nation!

Two years after the Northern Kingdom of Israel deemed the Word of God unbearable, the "Big One" hit. An earthquake of such shocking proportions rocked the land that for generations to come time was clocked from that fateful day.

C. 748 B.C. King Jeroboam II died. Zechariah, his son, reigned six months, then was murdered by the sword of Shallum. Thus the dynasty ended and anarchy began. Shallum ruled one month and was murdered by the next political aspirant, Menahem. So it went until the end—with uneasy reigns, royal assassinations and long interregnum periods (when the throne was up for grabs).

C. 745 B.C. Trouble brewed from an unexpected quarter. Assyria, long slumbering in the cradle of Mesopotamia, awoke. The soldier-usurper to the throne, Tiglath-Pileser III (Pulu, Pul), nursed its long-ailing armies back to health, fed the hungry nation visions of world conquest, cranked up the mighty Assyrian war machine and started rolling for points west.

Back on the home front, Israel had its hands full. A whirlwind

143

of chaos and confusion caught up the land. An epidemic of social ills debilitated its already weakened constitution. The "signs of the times" were those of a nation on its way out.

C. 734 B.C. The Assyrian war machine veered south. The Middle East seesaw teeter-tottered madly as Assyria rose sky high and Damascus fell (making Syria a tribute-paying province). In rapid succession, Hamath, Inyon, Abel and Dan were taken. Hazor was gutted and emptied of hope. Galilee was invaded; Transjordan lost.

The long walk began. Jewish captives were deported east of the Euphrates; other peoples were brought in to resettle the land. Tiglath-Pileser III died; Shalmaneser V replaced him. The trunk roads jammed with advancing Assyrian armies. Israelite troops fled. The common man scrounged for a place to hide.

C. 724 B.C. The siege of Samaria began. Shalmaneser V died; Sargon II replaced him. For three years Ms. Samaria (all that was left of the Northern Kingdom) lay broken and crushed upon her ground with none to help. For three years, the virgin of Israel died behind the walls, with famine, pestilence, disease and death her only companions.

Then came the end.

C. 721 B.C. Samaria fell, never to rise again.

In time, other peoples took her name and built upon her mounding ruins; but the once-great "nation under God," the high and mighty Northern Kingdom of Israel, was no more.

BY ORDER OF THE LORD